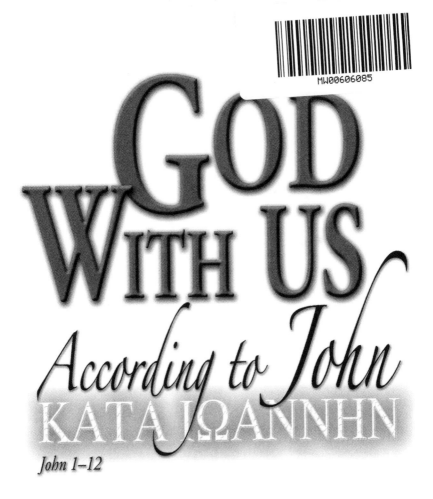

GOD WITH US
According to John
KATA ΙΩΑΝΝΗΝ

John 1–12

JAMES W. GILLEY

Pacific Press® Publishing Association
Nampa, Idaho
Oshawa, Ontario, Canada
www.pacificpress.com

3ABN BOOKS
PO Box 220, West Frankfort, Illinois
www.3ABN.org

Cover design by Steve Lanto
Cover art resources by iStockphoto.com
Inside design by Aaron Troia
Editing by Page One Communications

Additional copies of this book are available from two locations:
3ABN: Call 1-800-752-3226 or visit http://www.3ABN.org
Adventist Book Centers: Call 1-800-765-6955
or visit http://adventistbookcenter.com

3ABN Books is dedicated to bringing you the best in published materials consistent with the mission of Three Angels Broadcasting Network. Our goal is to uplift Jesus through books, audio, and video materials by our family of 3ABN presenters. Our in-depth Bible study guides, devotionals, biographies, and lifestyle materials promote the whole person in health and the mending of broken people. For more information, call 618-627-4651 or visit 3ABN's Web site: http://www.3ABN.org

ISBN 13: 978-0-8163-2285-5
ISBN 10: 0-8163-2285-6

08 09 10 11 12 • 5 4 3 2 1

GOD WITH US

DEDICATION

Lovingly dedicated to my daughter, Amy, her husband,
Ethan, and their son, Levi James

CONTENTS

INTRODUCTION

And truly Jesus did many other signs in the presence of His disciples, which are not written in this book; but these are written that you may believe that Jesus is the Christ, the Son of God, and that believing you may have life in His name.

—John 20:30, 31

This book is not a commentary; it is not a verse-by-verse study of this fantastic book of the New Testament. Many fine commentaries are available on the Gospel of John. Rather, the purpose of this book is to encourage you into deeper study of the Word of God and in particular, John's Gospel.

In this introduction and in chapter 1, I will provide some background information that could at times be a bit heavy for some. If it moves too slowly for you, just move on to chapter 2 and beyond. I've used a homiletic and practical approach to mine the truths of John as they affect everyday life. But here and there, sprinkling a few historical, theological, or philosophical tidbits may help in our understanding of the text. Don't worry that I will go too deep, since I do better when I can touch bottom myself!

Jesus had the greatest mind of all, able to present the deepest lessons in the simplest manner. Of purely human minds, I believe that John ranks right up there with Paul, Plato, Socrates, Philo, and the other great minds.

When you see the picture depicting John in *The Last Supper* painting by Leonardo da Vinci, you see a very delicate, quiet, mystical, smooth-faced, even effeminate person.

But a scriptural look at John shows just the opposite. In Mark 3:17, we see him as one of the " 'Sons of Thunder' "—a child of the storm against Roman occupation, a volatile spirit demonstrated when he joined with his brother James in demanding that Jesus bring " 'fire . . . down from heaven' " (Luke 9:54) to destroy those Samaritans who refused them entry into their village.

John was ambitious, as demonstrated when he and James accompanied their mother, Salome, as she made the famous request that her sons be placed one on the right-hand side and the other on the left-hand side—in the highest positions—when Christ would come into His kingdom (see Matthew 20:21).

But God can use a man like that! God would rather have a steamship plowing off course through the ocean at full speed, and then reset it, than a drifting hulk of steel with no direction or purpose or drive!

This fourth Gospel contains profound thoughts in the simplest language. Written originally in the most elementary Greek, John is usually the first or at least second book of the New Testament that students taking biblical Greek learn to read. And it has likely been read by more people than any piece of literature in all history.

The four Gospels are a presentation of the Deity—in Matthew, "Behold the King"; in Mark, "Behold the Servant"; in Luke, "Behold the Man"; and in John, "Behold Your God"! John is the great exponent of the Deity of Jesus Christ. As one man put it, "Looking at this book is like looking into the face of God."

John 20:31 tells us why it was written, "that you may believe that Jesus is the Christ, the Son of God, and that believing you may have life in His name." In this book, the word *believe* appears seventy times, but what does it really mean?

1. It means that you are convinced in your mind that Jesus is the Christ, the Son of God.
2. It means that you trust in your heart that everything He said is true. God does not lie!
3. It means that you commit your life to those two things in the Person of Christ—the Word, the True Logos.

You see, John was there at the baptism of Jesus. He heard John the Baptist say, "Behold the Lamb" and also heard the Voice from heaven, "This is My Beloved Son." He was at Cana for the first miracle; witnessed Christ's early Judean ministry; saw the resurrection of Lazarus; was present at the Lord's Supper, the trial of Jesus before Caiaphas, and the Crucifixion. And John was the first of the Twelve to believe in the Resurrection. Through John's eyes we too can "be there." Through his pages, we can discover beyond any doubt and believe that Jesus is God!

Chapter 1— John 1:1-18

THE ETERNAL CHRIST

This was one of those beautiful California days—a clear, blue sky—and you could actually see the mountains and hills nearby that you had heard were there but were seldom seen.

Camille and I drove up to a neat little house in Glendale that had been the home of Elder and Mrs. H. M. S. Richards Sr. for many years. Here, they had reared their four children. And from here, one of God's great but humble men had walked a mile or so every day to his Voice of Prophecy (VOP) office. He was known for always reading as he walked.

Earlier that day, at the close of a VOP counselor meeting at the media center in Thousand Oaks, he invited us to his home to see his library. He instructed me to follow his car, an ancient Chevy driven by his wife, Mabel. Because of an injury to his eye as a youth, Elder Richards never had adequate vision to drive. However, he had just enough vision to read instead of drive—and this gave him more time to read the ever-present book by his side.

Nonetheless, Mabel Richards could really drive—and drive she did! I lost her on the freeway; she could easily have been a NASCAR driver! The thought occurred to me that she must be trying to lose us! However, I quickly dismissed that, because she was such a gracious lady!

In time, we arrived and made our way to the backyard building that had been built for Elder Richards by close friends—such as the 1950s King's Heralds quartet, associate speaker Orville Iversen, and a few others. It was an unassuming place with no air conditioning and only a little space heater to take the chill off during colder weather as needed. As I remember, the desk was an uncomplicated board nailed to the wall with a support. Then there were the books, meticulously organized on simple shelves of unfinished lumber. The books were where his resources were spent—books were his passion.

Elder Richards was a great student of the Bible and the Spirit of Prophecy, and he, like Ellen White, had a large, wide-ranging library including books on theology and many other subjects of interest to him—especially biographies. Elder Richards knew that anyone who read a wide range of literature would find a combination of truth and error. This combination would allow the mining of truth away from the error—if they were properly anchored by the truth of God's Word and the inspired writings of the Spirit of Prophecy.

Many thoughts, stories, and experiences stand out in my mind from that Sunday afternoon we spent with Elder Richards in his library, but as a result of that visit, one special book of the Bible has through the years consistently influenced my walk with Christ.

Elder Richards grafted that onto my heart that afternoon, when he told me, "Jim, the book of John is where you need to study. The book of John is a good foundation for every sermon you preach." From that day, I've kept that as my focus, and although I've only delivered one complete series on the Gospel of John, it soon became the book to which I would return to repeatedly when seeking to share the truths of God's Word.

John's Gospel gave me a glimpse of who Jesus is and how to tell others of His love—especially in my most recent pastorate at the Dallas First SDA Church, just before coming to Three Angels

Broadcasting Network (3ABN). So now, as you read this book, I want to offer you some of the same insights I've shared with my beloved congregations and now with 3ABN viewers.

I want to challenge and urge you to dig into the Gospel of John. If you have—or want to get—a good study Bible, you'll be able to easily compare the verse you're studying with others and make notes. You can also expand your study through using the Spirit of Prophecy, as well as a couple of good commentaries.

Now, let's move right into John, chapter 1. These first eighteen verses are—and others agree with me—perhaps some of the greatest, most profound words of literature ever written. And here in these opening verses, John has three things he wanted his readers to notice.

First: Jesus is God in human flesh. The Incarnation says to us that Jesus is not just a reflection of God. He is not just Someone who looks like God. He IS God!

Sometimes people ask, "Are you monotheistic? Do you believe in one God?" Yes, I am—and I do! I am a "monotheist." I believe in one God—yet I believe in the Three, the Trinity: the Father, the Son, and the Holy Spirit. One—and yet Three. How can that be?

Well, let me tell you something, I can't explain how that is. Oh, I could give you all the different explanations people usually give—how the Members of the Trinity are One in purpose, for example. But I don't think any of those explanations actually do justice to the reality of who God is. I think for us to really understand it, we would have to *be* God.

So I think we have to be careful in trying to explain the Trinity. Believe it—yes! Fully understand it—no! I don't understand it. There are many things I see and believe but don't understand. I can say the same about many things I see in nature. Only a fool tries to explain everything in nature. So I'll not open my mouth and reveal my lack of knowledge!

God is God! Christ is God! And this is John's message—that God has come in the flesh.

Second: Jesus is not only God but the Savior of the world. He came to earth not just on a divine visit. He came for a purpose. He had an urgent mission—to save those He had created but who now desperately needed a Savior.

Third: The response of men and women to Christ's saving work. Some—perhaps most—rejected it. But some accepted it.

Some writers know just where to start. In writing Genesis, Moses knew where to start. So did John in writing his Gospel. They both began with the same words. Here's how John begins: "In the beginning was the Word," he wrote in verses 1 and 2, "and the Word was with God, and the Word was God. He was in the beginning with God."

In the beginning was the . . . *Logos*—the Greek word for "Word." But what is the meaning of *logos*? Why did John start out his Gospel by repeatedly using this word?

Part of the reason, at least, is that like all good writers, John knew that he should write with his main audience in mind. And for John, that meant mostly Greek converts to Christianity. Other Gospel writers spoke more directly to the Jews.

By the time John wrote, there were perhaps a thousand Greeks who accepted Christ for every Jew who did. So John may have thought to himself, *Well, look—why should my Greek readers have to understand the Messianic ideas of the Jews? Why should they have to understand Jesus and come to Him through Jewish Messianic philosophy?*

No, John chose to present Jesus in terms familiar to the Greeks. They were familiar with the concept of the Logos. They were familiar with the idea of a God who had always been. So John set his pen to the parchment and began, "In the beginning was the Word [*Logos*] . . ."

Every Greek would read that and say, "I know exactly what he's talking about—the Logos, the Power of the universe—God." They would say, "This is amazing!"

This brings me to Heraclitus—a Greek philosopher born in

535 B.C. who lived in Ephesus. He's the one who said that if you stepped into a river, stepped back out, and then stepped back in again, it wasn't the same river. The river had already passed by—and it was constantly changing.

Now, to a degree that's true. I mean, some things are always the same. I go out and get into my car. I've been getting into that car for a long time, and it hasn't changed. After 150,000 miles, it's still the same car.

But since so much in this universe—like the river he mentioned—does change, Heraclitus thought the universe would be nothing but chaos unless something was in control. And for Heraclitus, that power in control was the Logos—the Word. The concept of the Logos came to pervade Greek thought—and John knew it was an idea with which his readers would be immediately familiar.

Now quite a bit later, a Jewish philosopher came along named Philo (born in 20 B.C.)—and he worked to harmonize Greek and Jewish philosophies. Probably few men of his time understood the Hebrew Bible as fully as Philo did. Also, few understood Greek philosophy as Philo did.

And as Philo looked at Greek philosophy, he said, "This Logos, this idea of the Word, is talking about God. It is Yahweh—He is the Logos." So because of Philo's efforts to bring Greek and Jewish ideas together, when Jesus came, even the Jews were at least somewhat familiar with the idea of the Logos.

Now, as we take time to study John's Gospel (and by the way, when we study the Word of God, we really do need to just slow down and take our time), we find certain ideas that come through "loud and clear" right at the beginning.

One of those ideas is that Jesus didn't "begin" when He first arrived here on earth. He existed before that. In fact, John makes it clear that Jesus had *always* existed. Everything and everyone we know in this life has a beginning and an end. But that's not the case with God—He has always been, with no beginning. And

Jesus, therefore, also had no beginning, because, as John emphasized, Jesus is God.

So the preexistence of Jesus is one point John doesn't want his readers to miss. Another truth John doesn't want anyone to miss is that Jesus, the Word, was not only God, He was *with* God. The only way that could be true is if God was more than one person. And of course, if we let the Bible speak to us from cover to cover, that's exactly what we find—a God composed of Three Persons. Three Persons totally unified in thought, in character, and in purpose.

So totally in harmony are the Persons of the Trinity that no one can tell us more about God than Christ can. People may ask, "What is God like?" I'll tell you what God is like—He's like Christ. Somebody may protest, "But wait a minute, what about the God of the Old Testament?"

A little girl reading in the Old Testament one time found stories of all the battles and blood and said, "Well, you see, that was before God became a Christian."

We may laugh, but when you look at Christ, you understand God. God hasn't changed! But our comprehension of Him—our understanding of Him—changes when we see God as Jesus reveals Him to us.

"In the beginning was the Word, and the Word was with God, and the Word was God." Jesus is God. He was there from the beginning. So how do I know what God is like? Because of what Jesus reveals Him to be—that's how I know what God is like. The Word, John says, *was* God.

Now, if one of John's burdens was to be sure his readers knew that Jesus is God, he also wanted them not to miss that Jesus is also the Creator of the universe.

"All things were made through Him, and without Him nothing was made that was made" (John 1:3).

That's good enough to settle it for me. John spent all that time with Jesus, and he knew that he was spending time with the Creator of the universe. John was with Jesus, and he said (notice verse 3), "without Him nothing was made that was made." Do I believe that? Yes, I do—with all my heart I believe that!

By the way, John had spent time and energy fighting some heresies that arose in his time. One of those was Gnosticism. This philosophy taught the idea that matter and spirit were separate and in conflict. Gnostics taught that God was a spirit and that He was in conflict with matter. Their whole concept was that the creator of the physical world (matter) was therefore in conflict with the spirit realm which God ruled. So therefore, the creator they believed in could not be God.

But John said, "No—this is not true! The Creator and God are in harmony. In fact, they are one and the same. Jesus Himself is not only the Creator, He is God."

John has nailed down some vital points about Jesus in the first three verses of his Gospel:

- Jesus is the Word.
- Jesus has no beginning.
- Jesus is God.
- Jesus is also *with* God—a Member of the Trinity.
- Jesus is the Creator.

Next (see verse 4), John describes Jesus the Word in terms of life and light.

"In Him was life, and the life was the light of men. And the light shines in the darkness, and the darkness did not comprehend it" (verses 4, 5).

Have you ever been somewhere dark? I mean *really* dark. Suddenly, somebody lights a match. Does anybody in the room need to tell you where the light is? They comprehend it—there's light over there someplace, and they see it. So how is it that the Light came into the world, and men didn't comprehend it? Doesn't it seem that if a light begins to shine in darkness, everybody would see it?

I once heard a story that took place during World War II. During the war, sometimes whole cities would be blacked out so enemy planes couldn't see them easily from the air and drop their bombs. During one of those blackouts, a preacher said, "The blackout isn't going to stop our prayer meeting. We'll hold the service even in the dark."

But as the preacher spoke, someone in the totally dark room flipped on a light switch—and the preacher stopped preaching.

One man asked, "Why did he stop preaching?"

You see, that man was blind. He had no comprehension of light whatsoever. He didn't know that the lights had just come on. He was blind, just as the world to which Jesus came was spiritually blind. People were so blinded by legalism and rituals that they could not see Jesus. They could not comprehend Him. They were in the darkness—and when the light came, they did not comprehend it.

"There was a man sent from God, whose name was John. This man came for a witness, to bear witness of the Light, that all through him might believe" (verses 6, 7).

The "John" introduced here is not the John writing the Gospel but another John who also had known Jesus. In fact, Jesus was his Cousin. And this John—who came to be known as "John the Baptist"—was not the Light but was sent to bear witness of the Light.

John the disciple found it necessary to make this statement about John the Baptist. Why? Because too many had come to elevate John the Baptist to be equal, or nearly so, with the Messiah whose coming John announced.

Now, the Bible tells us that, among those born of women, none was greater than John the Baptist. He was as great as David, as great as Moses, as great as any of the prophets. He was the last of the Old Testament prophets and the first of the New Testament prophets. Quite a man, John. Yet John was just a man.

When you read the Gospel of John, it can almost seem that

John the disciple went out of his way to minimize the importance of John the Baptist. Why? Because people were elevating John the Baptist to a position virtually equal with Jesus. And he wasn't equal—not at all. Christ was the Word. He was the Savior. He was the Messiah. John was just the one chosen to herald the Messiah's coming—to usher Him in.

What a great responsibility! And to announce the Messiahship of His Son, God chose John. The Bible says that the Holy Spirit was in John even in his mother's womb. So John was indeed special.

But you know how it is. Some people began worshiping the proclaimer instead of the Messiah he came to announce. It's a human trait to begin giving allegiance to leaders we like. But John the disciple said, "Don't do it—he's just a man. There's no comparison."

And by the way, this was the message of John the Baptist himself. He kept saying, "Don't look at me. Don't follow me. Jesus must increase—and I must decrease." Notice what John the Baptist said about Jesus, beginning at verse 19:

> Now this is the testimony of John, when the Jews sent priests and Levites from Jerusalem to ask him, "Who are you?" He confessed, and did not deny, but confessed, "I am not the Christ." And they asked him, "What then? Are you Elijah?" He said, "I am not." "Are you the Prophet?" And he answered, "No." Then they said to him, "Who are you, that we may give an answer to those who sent us? What do you say about yourself?" He said: "I am
>
> 'The voice of one crying in the wilderness:
> "Make straight the way of the LORD," '
>
> as the prophet Isaiah said." Now those who were sent were from the Pharisees. And they asked him, saying,

"Why then do you baptize if you are not the Christ, nor Elijah, nor the Prophet?" John answered them, saying, "I baptize with water, but there stands One among you whom you do not know. It is He who, coming after me, is preferred before me, whose sandal strap I am not worthy to loose." These things were done in Bethabara beyond the Jordan, where John was baptizing (John 1:19–28).

The next day, John saw Jesus coming toward him, and he said, "Here's the Testimony—here's the Witness."

The witness of John the Baptist

In the Gospel of John, eight witnesses can be found concerning the Messiah. The first is the witness of John the Baptist. " 'Behold!' " John preached,

"The Lamb of God who takes away the sin of the world! This is He of whom I said, 'After me comes a Man who is preferred before me, for He was before me.' I did not know Him; but that He should be revealed to Israel, therefore I came baptizing with water." And John bore witness, saying, "I saw the Spirit descending from heaven like a dove, and He remained upon Him. I did not know Him, but He who sent me to baptize with water said to me, 'Upon whom you see the Spirit descending, and remaining on Him, this is He who baptizes with the Holy Spirit.' And I have seen and testified that this is the Son of God" (verses 29–34).

So the first witness is John the Baptist. And John the disciple says, "Yes, you love John the Baptist, but John the Baptist loves Jesus, because Jesus is the Messiah. Don't follow John—don't worship John. And follow John only if he leads you to Jesus."

The only time any of us should follow any preacher is when he's leading us to Jesus. If he's leading any other way, we should back away from him as far as we can, no matter how magnetic or entertaining he might be.

The witness of the Father

Then, John brings to view the witness of the Father. Jesus said, " 'And the Father Himself, who sent Me, has testified of Me' " (John 5:37). And again in John 8:18, " 'the Father who sent Me bears witness of Me.' "

The witness of Jesus Himself

Next, there's the witness of Jesus Himself. " 'Even if I bear witness of Myself, My witness is true' " (verse 14). And He said, " 'I am One who bears witness of Myself' " (verse 18).

The witness of Jesus' works

And then there's the witness of Christ's works. He said, " 'the works which the Father has given Me to finish . . . bear witness of Me' " (John 5:36). And many other verses speak of the works Jesus performed.

The witness of the Scriptures

The Scriptures, too, witness of Jesus: " 'Search the scriptures, for in them you think you have eternal life; and these are they which testify of Me' " (verse 39).

The witness of those who met Jesus

Those who met Jesus were also witnesses to Him. These included people such as the woman of Samaria, the woman at the well, the man who was born blind—and countless others.

The witness of the disciples

Among the most effective and credible witnesses to Jesus were the men who walked by His side through His ministry—His own disciples. " 'You also will bear witness, because you have been with Me from the beginning' " (John 15:27).

The witness of the Holy Spirit

Finally, the Holy Spirit—the Third Member of the Godhead—testified as a witness to Jesus: " 'When the Helper comes, . . . the Spirit of truth . . . , He will testify of Me' " (verse 26).

Eight witnesses or groups of witnesses. Anyone going to trial with that many witnesses would be at a great advantage.

Jesus didn't just show up on earth, claim to be the Messiah, and expect that His own claim would settle it for everyone. No, He had all these eight witnesses who joined as in one voice to support His claim to be the world's Messiah and Savior.

We've looked so far in this chapter at Jesus as the eternal Christ—the Word or Logos who had no beginning and will have no end. But in the first eighteen verses of John's first chapter, John also introduces us to other descriptions of Jesus Christ. In addition to being *the eternal Christ,* Jesus was also . . .

The unrecognized Christ: "That was the true Light which gives light to every man coming into the world. He was in the world, and the world was made through Him, and the world did not know Him. He came to His own, and His own did not receive Him" (John 1:9–11).

God chose the Jews as His people. He chose Abraham and said that from him, He would bring not only a great multitude but also the Messiah. So every Jewish mother wondered, as she gave birth to a male child, whether hers might be the promised Savior.

For centuries, the Jewish people looked for the Messiah. They talked about Him and studied about Him. Then, the Messiah came—and they didn't recognize Him! They didn't know Him. He came to them—and even His own did not receive Him.

The omnipotent Christ: "But as many as received Him, to them

He gave the right to become children of God, to those who believe in His name: who were born, not of blood, nor of the will of the flesh, nor of the will of man, but of God" (verse 12, 13).

The glorious Christ: "And the Word became flesh and dwelt among us, and we beheld His glory, the glory as of the only begotten of the Father, full of grace and truth. John bore witness of Him and cried out, saying, 'This was He of whom I said, "He who comes after me is preferred before me, for He was before me." ' And of His fullness we have all received, and grace for grace. For the law was given through Moses, but grace and truth came through Jesus Christ. No one has seen God at any time. The only begotten Son, who is in the bosom of the Father, He has declared Him" (verses 14–18).

No, we haven't seen God the Father, but we've seen Jesus—and because we've seen Him, we know what God is like.

When Moses talked with God, the Bible tells us he was talking with Christ. Christ was the One in the cloud that went before Israel. Christ was the One in the pillar of fire by night. And as Moses spoke with Him, he asked to see God's glory. But God said No. "You can't look on Me in My present form," He told Moses. "It would destroy you."

But God told Moses that He would hide him in the cleft of a rock and show him just a glimpse of His glory. So Moses stepped into the cleft of the rock, and God shielded Moses as He passed by and gave Moses a brief glimpse of His glory. And the Bible says that even that brief glimpse caused Moses' face to shine as he descended from the mountain.

That same glorious God wants to have a personal friendship with you—a growing, real, deepening relationship. That same God is the One who came to this earth and became flesh—one of us in form.

And as you get to know Jesus, like Moses, you'll want to see more of Him. You'll want to see more of His glory—His character of love. And in His Word, He will reveal Himself to you.

It's likely that no one on earth came to know Jesus as well as did the disciple John. Since that's true, who else but Christ's closest human friend could be better able to tell us what Jesus is really like?

As Pastor Richards said to me, "The book of John—that's where you need to study." So join me as we spend time learning from John in the chapters ahead.

Chapter 2 — John 1:19–31

VOICE IN THE WILDERNESS

Now this was John's testimony when the Jews of Jerusalem sent priests and Levites to ask him who he was. He did not fail to confess, but confessed freely, "I am not the Christ."

They asked him, "Then who are you? Are you Elijah?"

He said, "I am not."

"Are you the Prophet?"

He answered, "No."

Finally they said, "Who are you? Give us an answer to take back to those who sent us. What do you say about yourself?"

John replied in the words of Isaiah the prophet, "I am the voice of one calling in the desert, 'Make straight the way for the Lord.'"

Now some Pharisees who had been sent questioned him, "Why then do you baptize if you are not the Christ, nor Elijah, nor the Prophet?"

"I baptize with water," John replied, "but among you stands one you do not know. He is the one who comes after me, the thongs of whose sandals I am not worthy to untie."

This all happened at Bethany on the other side of the Jordan, where John was baptizing.

The next day John saw Jesus coming toward him and said, "Look, the Lamb of God, who takes away the sin of the world! This is the one I meant when I said, 'A man who comes after me has surpassed me

*because he was before me.' I myself did not know him, but the reason
I came baptizing with water was that he might be revealed to Israel."*
—John 1:19–31, NIV

One thing is sure: we don't know a whole lot about John the Baptist, but from what we do know, he was definitely unique—and beyond question, one of the most fascinating men in all the Bible.

We know, of course, that he didn't dress as other people did. Like Tarzan, he wore skins everywhere—even while preaching. I'm sure that would create a real stir today—to have the preacher up front preaching in animal hides!

We also know that his diet was, to say the least, a bit peculiar. The Bible says he ate locusts and honey. Scholars have debated about the locusts, some suggesting they were of the "bug" variety with legs and wings; others of the opinion that they were the seeds in the pods of the carob tree.

Some believe that John couldn't have eaten locusts, since "bugs" are unclean—and of all people, John wouldn't have eaten anything unclean.

You know, it honestly could have been either one. Apparently, Jewish dietary laws provided that the Levites were exempt from some restrictions, so since John was a Levite, perhaps he was free to have bugs for breakfast. Also, some of the dietary laws *did* allow for eating certain insects.

Having spent a lot of time in that part of the world, I haven't seen enough locusts of the bug variety to keep anybody alive. But over there, you do see plenty of locusts of the vegetarian variety, so I personally suspect that's what John ate.

What we know about John the Baptist, we learn in bits and pieces. It's kind of like when you're in the Middle East, and you come upon some of the ruins there, and you see part of a wall or a partial column, and you begin to put the puzzle together. You can sort of imagine what it might have once looked like by picking up fragments lying around. That's what we have as a picture of John. We know a little about how he dressed and what he ate. We know a little bit about his imprisonment. We know that he had a moment of doubt. We know that John later died, and we know how that happened.

But when we look closely at John the Baptist, we realize that here was a man who knew who he was. That much is clear beyond question. So when people came to him and tried to give him lofty titles, he said, "No, I'm not that person."

"Are you that prophet?" they asked.

"No."

"Then who are you?"

In essence, John is saying, don't be all focused on who I am. That isn't what matters. What matters is that I'm just a voice, crying in the wilderness. It's *what I have to say* that matters.

And you know what? That's exactly how it should be as we share our message today.

As Seventh-day Adventist Christians, we are not out to build stars out of people—at least, we *shouldn't* be out to build stars out of people. Anyone who teaches or preaches or leads or evangelizes—and anyone (which includes all of us) who shares the good news with anyone else—should point people only in one direction—toward Jesus Christ.

John's whole ministry was to point people to Jesus and prepare people for His first coming. That was his job, and he did it well. He said, " 'He [Jesus] must increase, but I must decrease' " (John 3:30). John said, "The One coming after me is so great that I'm not even good enough to reach down and untie His shoe for Him. He is the only One who is great!"

John truly understood himself—and that produced in him genuine humility. Now, sometimes we get the idea that humility is really weakness. But who can possibly ever say John was weak? It's not someone weak who stands true, even if it means ending up in jail. It's not someone weak who stands by the truth, even if it results in his own death.

Imagine yourself living in John's time, and you run into a friend.

"Have you been down there to hear John preach?"

"Yes, I have."

"Well, what did he say?"

"Oh, listen—I have never heard anybody preach like that man! He talked about wheat and chaff and fire burning up the chaff."

"He said that?"

"And he showed a lot of courage when the Pharisees and Sadducees showed up. You know what he said to them? 'You generation of vipers.' "

"He said that to them?"

"Yes, he really said that, right to their faces."

Now, here's a side of John that some might not think seems very humble. We get this idea that humility means you let everybody walk on you—and it doesn't mean that at all. What it means for us as Christians is that we understand, as John did, the mission God has given to each of us. It means that we understand that—as we look at ourselves in comparison with God— He is far greater than we are. There is no comparison! That is true humility.

Do you remember the *Readers Digest* feature, "The Most Unforgettable Character I Ever Met"? If I had ever written an article for that feature, it would have been about Ray Rushing—a preacher I met during my unsuccessful political campaign back in the 1970s. I took temporary leave of my senses and ran for the United States Congress. Good experience for a young man—I learned a lot and met a lot of people but would never do it again. And thank the Lord, I was not elected. Believe me, I'm not running for anything—or from anybody!

I had never met another man quite like him. He was much like I would imagine John the Baptist to have been, literally, except that he wore fine suits and drove a nice car. But he was not afraid to speak his mind. He was the editor of *The National Voice,* a temperance quarterly, and he was not afraid to take on the liquor lobby or anyone else that he thought was polluting America.

I remember the first time I ever spent any time with him—we went to a restaurant. We sat down, and I was about to do as I usually do—bow my head quietly and silently ask God's blessing on my food.

Let me interrupt here to tell you about another time when I did that, with unexpected results. I had bowed my head, and suddenly a waitress whizzed past, removed my plate, and said, "Don't look at those eggs like that—we'll cook them over."

"No," I protested, "I wasn't looking at the eggs. I was just . . ." But she'd already gone! It had taken a long time to get those eggs in the first place, and now I had to wait to get them all over again.

But let me finish now with my meeting with this modern-day John the Baptist. As I bowed my head, suddenly a booming voice from the other side of the table spoke up: "Heavenly Father, we thank You for this food, we thank You for the blessings You've given us, and we thank You in Jesus' name. Amen."

The whole restaurant fell silent. Waiters stopped midstride, and patrons stopped chewing! Everybody in the restaurant now had their food blessed, whether they had asked for it or not! I thought to myself, *I wonder if he does this all the time.*

I ate a lot of meals with Ray through the years after that, and he did it every single time. "I'm not ashamed of the gospel of Christ," he told me. He only knew one way to pray—and that was with his volume set on "loud and clear." Sometimes I wanted to say to him, "Ray, the Lord can hear the still, quiet voice." But I don't think that Ray ever thought that was true. In addition, he would always leave an outrageously large tip! "They know I'm a preacher," he would say, "and I don't want them to think that preachers are cheapskates!"

Sometimes, he would come to my office, walk right in, and

say, "Jim, the Lord has laid a burden on my heart, and I need to come here and pray with you about it."

I'd say, "Let's pray," and we'd get down on our knees, and he would start to pray. Now, I will tell you something: when Ray prayed for you, you knew you'd been prayed for! Believe me!

One day he came to me and said, "I'm going to take you to Austin. I want you to meet the governor."

"Let's go," I said.

We got in the car and drove down to Austin, the Texas State capital. As we walked up to the governor's secretary, I asked, "Did you get us an appointment?"

"No," he replied, "I don't have to get an appointment."

"Are you sure?" I asked.

"I'm sure."

He then walked up to the governor's secretary and said, "Tell the governor that Ray Rushing is here."

"Do you have an appointment?" she asked.

"I don't need an appointment," Ray assured her. "You just tell him Ray Rushing is here."

In less than three minutes, we were in the governor's office. So I had learned this amazing secret. You see, governors don't have a thing to do! They just sit around all the time waiting for people to come and see them. And here all this time I had thought they were busy!

Anyway, we went in, sat down, and talked with the governor. There, the governor poured out his heart to Ray. The governor was wrestling with a big personal problem. So we got on our knees in the governor's office and prayed for him. And I want you to know that the governor knew he'd been prayed for when Ray finished praying for him.

Ray got to his feet and said to me, "Now I want you to meet the lieutenant governor."

"I'd like that," I told him.

So we went over to the lieutenant governor's office. As it happened, he too was facing a real problem in his life. Some months before, he and his wife had separated and later divorced, and it had come as a big shock to him.

Next stop was the U.S. senator's Austin office, and it happened he was in town from Washington. Again, in just moments, we were visiting with him in his private office—and without an appointment.

Everyplace Ray went, they knew him. They knew who he was, but more importantly, they knew *what* he was. They knew that the number one thing in his life was the gospel of Jesus Christ. And he walked unafraid with all kinds of people. You might see him with the lowliest of the low, helping people of whom he sometimes said, "They aren't even housebroken, much less church-broken! But we try to help them, anyway."

Ray was ready to reach out to that kind of person—or to the one holding the highest office in the state. Either one, it didn't matter to him. Ray opened door after door after door for me, so I could become acquainted with these people with great responsibilities. He even introduced me to then Treasury Secretary John Connally, who as Texas governor was riding in the car when President Kennedy was assassinated. He himself was seriously wounded.

There were many others, including Medal of Honor recipient Joe Foss. When I met him, Joe had recently served as governor of South Dakota. He was living in Phoenix, Arizona, and Ray took me over to meet him.

Some of you may know that some consider Joe Foss to have been the greatest—and perhaps most-decorated—American hero of World War II. My personal choice for that would be Desmond Doss.

When we met Joe, he said, "I'll pick you up early tomorrow morning, I want you to go to a prayer breakfast with me."

At the prayer breakfast, we met all kinds of folks I'd never met before. One of them was the famous major league umpire Jocko

Conlin. Conlin is especially known for his verbal battles with Leo Durocher, manager of the New York Giants. When I met him, I found that he wore thick glasses. Now, I had never seen him wear glasses while he was umpiring, so I said something to him about it—and he just laughed.

"I never saw you wearing those when you were calling balls and strikes for the World Series on television," I said.

"I can see either way—with or without them. It doesn't matter," he replied as he laughed. *Blind either way,* I thought.

After my campaign was over, I thought I'd never see Ray again, but later, he showed up one day at my door.

"You've got to get back closer to preaching," he told me. "You're not preaching enough—you're too involved with business. I know about a little business near here that works with churches. It would be ideal for you. That business could support you, and you could preach."

"Ray," I protested, "I don't need another business. I can barely hold on to the one I have." At the time, I had a promotional advertising firm.

"I can barely keep this operation going," I said.

"Well, I want you to see this business," Ray insisted.

"I'm sorry, Ray," I said, "but I'm just not interested in it."

But about that same time, Pastor Lee Huff came to me—the pastor of the Dallas church—and he said the same thing to me. I repeated to him that I wasn't interested. Then the associate pastor came to me with the same idea. No, I said again—not interested.

Soon after this, Ray called me again and said, "I want you to go out there."

"No," I said firmly. "I won't do it."

Finally one day, Ray called me and said he wanted to take me to lunch. Now, I often accept invitations to lunch! So I said Yes.

Ray got me in the car, and I didn't know where we were going. So I said, "Ray, where are we going? I don't have much time—and you're going way out here in the country."

"I just have to make a stop," he said.

When we pulled into the parking lot, I knew I had been tricked. Ray took me right up to the door of a place where I was to spend the next thirteen years of my life with a business called Missionary Tape and Equipment Supply. Ray took me in and introduced me to the owner, and to make a long story short, some four or five months later I ended up with that business, because Ray took me there.

This organization became the base from which my wife, Camille, and our four children—Jim Jr., Maryann, John, and Amy—held forty-three full, four-week evangelistic series during the next ten years. This organization paid all our personal expenses, so the meetings cost the conference a portion of the local budget only.

I've seen Ray reach out to so many people and help them. He was a man with a great heart for people. I remember one time when a friend of mine, Les, was having a terrible financial problem. It was two days before Christmas, so Ray went to Les and told him, "Don't worry about that financial problem—don't worry about it. Just enjoy Christmas, and I'll share the solution with you after the Christmas holidays."

"Ray," I asked, "you don't have the money to solve Les's problem. How are you going to take care of it?"

"I've just turned it over to the Lord," Ray told me. "I didn't want him to worry all during the holidays. I wanted him to have a good weekend. He's worrying too much—he's worrying himself sick."

"But Ray," I said, "he's still going to have to face this next week."

"Well then," Ray answered, "we'll face it next week, and we'll face that problem with the Lord. The Lord will give an answer. I've already given it to the Lord, and I've already claimed the victory, and He's already given us the answer."

"Do you know what the answer is?" I asked him.

"NO!" Ray said. "But that's not important, because the Lord knows what it is."

And the next week when we got together, the Lord did give the answer.

Now, Ray was, I believe, the kind of man John the Baptist was. He was strong. He had a saying he'd use sometimes when things really got heated with somebody: "Look, I'll pray with you or I'll fight you—either one. You just say whichever one it is. I prefer to pray with you. But I won't back down from anything." And he wouldn't. A slogan he had on his calling card said, "Praise the Lord, anyhow!" In other words, even if you don't think your prayers are being answered.

Ray used to call our house, and while what he'd say some might not think was very humble, I think it showed his sense of humor and that he didn't take himself too seriously. He'd call our house, and when my daughter would answer the phone, he'd ask, "Who is this?"

"Amy."

"Well, Amy, you tell your daddy that the world's greatest preacher is on the phone!" I always knew immediately who it was. Ray would walk into a group of people and say to them, "You asked for a blessing, and here I am." And everyone would laugh; it was the way he would warm up the group.

One day Ray's wife called me and said, "Jim, last Friday afternoon, Ray died. He went to sleep in Jesus, and even though as a Baptist Ray knew a thousand Baptist preachers, he wanted you to be one of the two pastors to conduct his funeral."

Ray and I had studied the Sabbath together, and he accepted this truth and started keeping the Sabbath on his own. He went to the renowned pastor of the large Baptist church where his membership was located and told him that he believed that the Sabbath was still binding on Christians. This pastor agreed with Ray.

"Then why don't you keep it?" Ray asked, and this pastor indicated that indeed he did, neither buying nor selling nor doing anything secular on that day. When Ray asked him why he didn't tell the congregation about the Sabbath truth, this famous pulpiteer, known around the world, responded by telling Ray that he had been the pastor of the church for forty-six years and was hoping to reach fifty years—and that if he told the congregation on Sunday morning the truth about the Sabbath, that by Sunday night he would be fired as their pastor by the board of deacons.

When Ray had told his wife he wanted me to be one of the pastors to conduct his funeral, he said, "Because I want to see the look on Dr. W's face when he sees that I have a Seventh-day Adventist minister to conduct my funeral!" Now even though I had convinced Ray on the Sabbath, I had not done a very good job on the state of the dead! He still held a Baptist view on that, unfortunately!

At the funeral, for my part of the program, I simply shared a few experiences, some quite humorous, that Ray and I had enjoyed as we had been praising the Lord together. I prayed more with that man than with any other human being, outside of my family. I never once saw him step back from his witness as a Christian. Through some tough personal times, he had always put Christ first. It was a great honor to be asked to speak at his funeral.

Ray had three sons and a daughter. And through the years, I had observed how much they loved and admired their dad. I can nearly always tell what kind of person someone is by what their children think of them. You see, our children see us when we're home. They see us when all pretense is gone. I knew how this man's kids loved him.

They came to me after the funeral and each of them hugged me and thanked me—three grown sons and a grown daughter. They said, "We're glad you put a little life in this funeral today, because Daddy would have wanted it that way."

John the Baptist was a humble man. A strong man. Jesus said

of him that there was none greater born of woman than John the Baptist. If we accept Jesus Christ, put Him first in our lives, and proclaim Him as Savior, then, my friend, we're fulfilling the commission Christ gave us, pointing the way to Him. That's our job—pointing people to Jesus, just as John the Baptist did.

A friend from the General Conference told me years ago that he went to see one of the greatest preachers of our time.

"When I walked in and started to listen to this man," he said, "I couldn't take my eyes off him. He was dressed impeccably. His speech was impeccable. He had tremendous ideas that he put together one after the other till I was totally amazed by it."

But then, my friend said, another man came to town.

"I went to see him, and when I saw him walk out to the pulpit, I was totally unimpressed with him physically—totally unimpressed. But when he began to speak, he began to talk of Jesus. It's a good thing I had noticed him at first," my friend told me, "because once he started speaking of Jesus, that was the last time I saw him. From then on, I could only see Jesus."

John the Baptist pointed people to Jesus. Your job—my job—is simply to point our friends, our family members, the people we meet, to Jesus. He will take care of the rest.

Chapter 3 — John 2:13–35

THE STRONG SON OF GOD

When it was almost time for the Jewish Passover, Jesus went up to Jerusalem. In the temple courts he found men selling cattle, sheep and doves, and others sitting at tables exchanging money. So he made a whip out of cords, and drove all from the temple area, both sheep and cattle; he scattered the coins of the money changers and overturned their tables. To those who sold doves he said, "Get these out of here! How dare you turn my Father's house into a market!"

His disciples remembered that it is written: "Zeal for your house will consume me."

Then the Jews demanded of him, "What miraculous sign can you show us to prove your authority to do all this?"

Jesus answered them, "Destroy this temple, and I will raise it again in three days."

The Jews replied, "It has taken forty-six years to build this temple, and you are going to raise it in three days?" But the temple he had spoken of was his body. After he was raised form the dead, his disciples recalled what he had said. Then they believed the Scripture and the words that Jesus had spoken.

Now while he was in Jerusalem at the Passover Feast, many people saw the miraculous signs he was doing and believed in his name. But Jesus would not entrust himself to them, for he knew all men. He did not need man's testimony about man, for he knew what was in a man.

—*John 2:13–24, NIV*

Some artist's illustrations of Jesus, I just can't accept. Jesus—weak and emaciated. Or effeminate. Or dressed in spotless white, His hair and beard perfectly styled and in place.

Sorry—that just isn't the Jesus I picture. Jesus was a carpenter, after all. Muscular and well-built. He spent his life mostly in the outdoors. Tanned, rugged, weathered. He lived in a place of dust and heat. So He wore what people wore then—and still do in that part of the world. Nobody wears white in a land of hot, dusty winds.

No, Jesus wasn't sanitized and styled or effeminate, either in appearance or manner. He spent His life in a place that builds hard, strong, energetic people. And Jesus was strong not just physically—He also was strong from the inside. When Jesus came to the temple, He came with an inner power no one could ignore.

The message of John's Gospel is that the Jesus John knew is God! Jesus was not just a good teacher. He was not just a good example. If the most important concern of Jesus was to be a role model, it certainly didn't help that He hung out with drunkards and prostitutes. And Jesus was no odd, crazy fanatic from Nazareth with delusions of being God.

Jesus wasn't a fanatic. Fanatics attract followers, but in time people grow disillusioned with their teachings and actions. Not Jesus. His disciples were willing to die for Him.

And Jesus was not a phony. A phony doesn't ultimately come back from the dead. He was no phantom. You can't nail a phantom to a cross. He was not a myth. History doesn't center on a myth. The calendar does not divide history between the time before and after . . . a myth.

John's message was that Jesus was God in a human body. Jesus, John begins his book, was there in the beginning. He was the Creator. And John insists that in saying these things, he's not alone. Andrew says the same thing, John says. So does Philip. And Nathanael. And what about Mary—Jesus' mother? She asked Jesus to perform a miracle—to do what only God could do, to create! And at Cana, Jesus did just that.

But now as we see Jesus through John's eyes, we come to a time in the life of Jesus that once again confirmed that Jesus was indeed God. It's the time of the Passover, and Jerusalem is crowded with the faithful. A constant din of loud noise—voices, animals, and the clink and clatter of coins—fills the temple courtyard. And the courtyard was no small space—it occupied a full fourteen acres. Jesus walked right into this multitude. He found a length of rope and quickly made a whip of it.

Now, we have no record that Jesus ever actually struck anyone, and I'm sure He didn't. That would be utterly out of harmony with His character. But His eyes flashed with indignation as He held that makeshift whip in His hand. His eyes swept over the scene: livestock and doves for sale, to be used as Passover sacrifices . . . tables bearing various coins . . . money changers shouting and bargaining and intimidating buyers in order to maximize their profits.

Suddenly Jesus, His eyes flashing, walked over to a nearby table and turned it over. Coins scattered loudly in all directions over the hard bricks. The crowd fell silent. Jesus walked from table to table, upending each of them, as His voice echoed off the courtyard walls: " 'It is written, . . . "My house will be called a house of prayer," but you are making it a "den of robbers" ' " (Matthew 21:13, NIV).

The crowd dispersed; the money changers ran in panic.

Now, it's true that with pilgrims converging on Jerusalem from all over to celebrate Passover— as well as those living in the city— a legitimate need existed to exchange currencies. The normal coin in use was the Roman coin. But there would also have been coins from Egypt, Greece, and other countries. Since these coins bore the face of the Roman emperor, they could not be used in the temple—there, special Hebrew temple coins were required. So an exchange was needed—nothing wrong with that.

If you've ever traveled to a foreign country, you know that when you change your money, you "get skinned" by the exchange fees—and when you change it back, the same thing happens. So you try not to change it very often, since you pay both ways. That happened in Christ's time—and it still happens today.

But at that time, something else was taking place. All kinds of animals to be sacrificed were available: cattle, sheep, doves, and others. The money changers and animals for sale could have been located outside the temple courtyard, respecting the sacredness of God's "house of prayer." But instead, the animals and their sellers, along with the money changers, set up their operation right inside the temple courtyard, like some giant outdoor flea market. Fourteen acres of bustle and hustle, backed right up to the doors of the Holy Place.

Understandably, people traveling from a great distance didn't want to carry animals to sacrifice—even a couple of doves—all those long miles. So they said, "We'll just wait till we get there and buy a dove or an animal to sacrifice." So of course, meeting this need created a booming business during Passover time in Jerusalem.

But doves that might usually only cost, say, two for a dime, were being marked up and sold two for four dollars. The greedy sellers and money changers were gouging and ripping off customers unopposed—a nearly unbearable burden for the poor.

Caiaphas, the son-in-law of Annas, was the high priest. His four sons were really in control of the temple at that time. And selling sacrificial animals had become a wildly successful money-making scheme—they were cleaning up!

Let's say that you are a sincere Israelite back then, and you have a lamb you've raised—fed it and cared for it till it's almost like a pet. To you this is a special lamb, not just one you've randomly chosen out of your flock. You take it to the temple intending to offer your lamb as your Passover sacrifice.

"Have you seen the inspector yet?" someone asks you.

"Well, no—I haven't."

"Then you'll need to see the inspector, because your lamb has to be perfect and pass inspection to be used in the service."

"But my lamb *is* perfect," you protest.

You take it to the inspector, who quickly looks it over.

"I don't like the looks of this lamb's eyes," he says. "And this foot is a bit soft here. I can't let this lamb pass inspection."

"So what am I going to do?" you ask.

"Well, right over here we have lambs for sale that have already passed inspection."

You look at the price, and your mouth opens in disbelief.

Noticing your reaction, the inspector says, "You can go home and get another lamb to bring back if you wish. Do whatever you want—but your lamb isn't going to be used in the sacrifice."

So you go over and choose one of the preapproved lambs and buy it.

After you've offered it in sacrifice, you come back—and there, over in the pen full of approved lambs for sale, you see your lamb! They've ripped you off! And these merchants continued ripping off people in the temple courtyard till they had heaped up huge profits for themselves.

You know, God hates sin. And if you look at Scripture, it's clear that the sin God hates most is religious sin—hypocrisy. If you look at Scripture, you find that Christ was always ready to welcome and forgive the sinner. He lifted up and encouraged the woman who had fallen into adultery. But one thing is for sure: Jesus never condoned those who knew better, profiting from the gospel.

Against the background of this story of the money changers, I want to put in a plug right here for our denomination. We're not perfect, and I don't think anybody in our denomination would tell you that we are. However, I'm convinced that if we make any mistake, it's that we underpay our preachers. With the cost of living these days, it's a definite challenge for our pastors. And I know that they work hard for whatever they receive. No one should wonder about that—nearly all pastors I know put in far longer hours than those with nine-to-five jobs.

Pastors make mistakes. They're quite obviously human. But they're certainly not in it for the money—that, I'll guarantee. They wouldn't be in this denomination and doing this work, if they were in it for the money. And in our church, if you go up the ladder, you find that there, they make very little more. The difference between what the General Conference president and the pastor of a local church make would likely be only a few thousand dollars a year. Our pastors can never successfully be accused of profiting from the gospel.

I think the time is coming when we need to raise our pastors' salaries. I really do. The only way they can survive today is if their wives also work. It takes wives working and kids that don't eat (just kidding) and just a lot of things to come together just right, for pastors to make it these days. They have to both work, in most cases, to make it. We need to do far more to support our pastors.

Two friends of mine shared an interesting experience with me. Recently they traveled to the East Coast and visited a large church of another denomination that has a large television ministry—a big independent ministry. The pastor there gets whatever he wants—I mean anything.

My friends learned that a couple of weeks before their visit, he told his church to go out and get him the best BMW they could find. He already had some other big cars at home, but he wanted a BMW with every available option on it—all the bells and whistles. And they got it for him!

While my friends were there, they were talking with this pastor, and he stopped his financial man, who was walking by, and said, "Hey, tell everybody I appreciated that BMW—and that I want another one next week just like it, for my wife."

You talk about money! I don't know what BMWs go for, but I know it's serious money.

Not long ago, I was talking with a man of another denomination.

"How much do the ministers in the Seventh-day Adventist Church make?" he asked. So I told him, and he looked at me in total disbelief.

"I can't believe that," he said.

"So what does a minister in your church make?" I asked.

"Our ministers are not on a set salary," he replied.

"Oh, really?" I replied, "Then what are they on—a commission?"

"No, they're on a percentage."

"What's the percentage?" I asked.

"Sixty percent of the tithe," he said. "For a church of four hundred members that would be about two hundred and forty thousand dollars a year in salary."

From where I look at it, that's a lot of profiting from the gospel—a LOT of profiting from the gospel.

I talked not long ago with the treasurer of a large charismatic church in Texas about how much the pastor of their church made. He told me that they reported the pastor's salary at one hundred thousand dollars a year. Naïvely, I said, "Well, considering what all these other guys get, I guess one hundred thousand dollars a year isn't all that much."

"But his salary doesn't include his housing allowance," the treasurer told me.

"So how much is his housing allowance?" I asked, thinking it might be ten thousand dollars or twenty thousand dollars a year.

"It's two hundred and forty thousand dollars a year," he said.

Somehow, in many congregations today, the thinking of the members has been turned upside down and sideways. They've been led to think that the more their preacher gets, the better. That's just plain brainwashing, as I see it. Many of those members are fighting just to get by, and meanwhile, their pastor is up there telling them he needs another BMW!

Money changers in the temple of God! I'll tell you something, though—God knows how to handle it. At the temple, Jesus handled it before, and He'll handle it again today.

When Jesus saw this sin which He hates, He moved to do something about it. He told them His temple was for praying—not preying. But even then, some of them had the gall to ask Him, " 'What miraculous sign can you show us to prove your authority to do all this?' " (John 2:18, NIV).

Jesus didn't have to answer them—not even one word. But He did anyway. And we need to notice carefully what He said, because nothing Jesus ever said was trivial or unimportant. His words were so deep that even today as we read them, we can read them once, ten times, or a hundred—and each time we'll find new insights we'd missed before.

Jesus said, " 'Destroy this temple, and in three days I will raise it up' " (verse 19).

The religious leaders almost choked on their derision. " 'It has taken forty-six years to build this temple, and will You raise it up in three days?' " (verse 20).

But, the Bible says, Jesus was speaking of the temple of His body. The Jews all came to Jerusalem, because that is where the temple was. That was supposed to be the residence of God. So where is God's temple today? Is it our church world headquarters? Is it the local church building where you go for services on the weekend?

God may be present in these places, but the Bible is clear that today, His temple is . . . *you!* Jesus lives in the hearts of men, women, and children—in you, and in me.

So Jesus was telling them something quite literally, when He said, " 'Destroy this temple, and in three days I will raise it up' " (verse 19). Yes, He said, you will destroy this temple (meaning Himself). But in doing that, you'll also be destroying this temple in Jerusalem that you've desecrated.

You remember what the Bible says happened at the moment Jesus died on the cross—the veil in the temple between the Holy Place and the Most Holy Place was ripped apart from top to bottom. This was God's way of signaling that the sacrificial system—from His viewpoint, at least—was over. Some evidence exists that the Jewish people continued it anyway, but it no longer had any meaning. They had destroyed the temple of Christ's body. And in so doing, they destroyed their treasured temple in Jerusalem—it was left to them desolate.

I have a good friend who is a Jew, and I enjoy this man's company. He's our guide when we visit Israel. Sometimes when he talks about the rebuilding of the temple, we have asked him, "What are you going to sacrifice if you ever rebuild the temple— what kind of sacrifice will you do?" And he's always silent.

The world has changed today. People value animals differently than they did centuries ago. Today, if animal sacrifices began again, without doubt, it would create a huge uproar. We love our animals these days. In fact, in some homes, the dogs and cats get far more love than the people there seem to get.

I remember we had a little dog once—a little puppy named Abbey. We all loved Abbey—especially my daughter Amy. Abbey was *her* dog. Well, one morning I was happily going off to work. I got in my car and drove down the driveway. My driveway went straight down and then turned to the right. So I followed the driveway and as usual, turned to the right. What I didn't know was that Abbey was running alongside the car, and when I turned to the right, bless her little heart, I ran right over her, and she was so tiny I didn't even know it.

When I got to the office, one of my employees was standing

out in front and said to me angrily, "Get back home—you've run over the dog."

"What do you mean, I ran over the dog? I never felt a thing." I'm already guilty—how do they know I'm the one who did it?

"Listen, you'd better get back home. There's quite a thing going on back there."

When I got back, everybody was crying. I *had* run over Abbey. I tried to figure out some other way Abbey might have died, but came up empty. I couldn't stand the way Amy looked at me with those eyes that said, "Daddy, how *could* you?"

I didn't know that I had run over Abbey—yet with my family, I was guilty of her death even if it was an accident! Can you imagine how hard it would be for me to deliberately kill an animal? Even if it were for a religious sacrifice? Do you think today that people could stretch out a lamb that's become a pet—almost a member of the family—and slit its throat? We live in a totally different time now.

The temple service is over. It no longer has meaning. But when they destroyed the temple of Jesus' own body, in three days, Jesus came forth again, just as He had promised and predicted. The Jerusalem temple was no longer where He would dwell. Now He would live in human hearts.

The Jews had asked, "What sign can You give us?" Unbelief is always looking for a sign. Unbelief is always looking for a miracle. Unbelief is always saying, "Do another trick." That's unbelief. Belief simply says, "I trust You. I commit myself to You." And the Bible says that Jesus knew their hearts, and because they would not commit to Him, neither would He commit to them.

You and I may know all about Jesus. But there's a difference between knowing about Jesus and committing fully to Him. Sometimes I've had the beautiful experience of bringing somebody to Jesus who has known Him all their life. They've known all about Him, they've believed in Him, but they've never committed themselves to Him. They've never said, "Lord, I am

Yours—one hundred percent Yours. I am no longer mine. I belong to You. Take me and use me as You wish."

Those who make that commitment have the sure promise of the resurrection, should they reach the end of life before Jesus comes back. Someday, that's going to happen, you know. Someday soon, Jesus will come back because after three days, He came out of that tomb. He will come back for all who have offered themselves to be His temples here on earth—offering to Him their own bodies, in and through which He can live out His life everyday.

If you have any "money changers" in your heart—greed, anger, lust, envy, hatred, resentment—any of those attitudes and habits that shouldn't be there, Jesus can drive them out. Give Him permission, and He'll cleanse your heart-temple so He can live there. And if You let Him, He will come in and live in you right now.

And for the rest of this day.

And tomorrow.

And till your last breath.

And then after the resurrection—forever.

Chapter 4 — John 3:1–15

MAN'S GREATEST NEED

Now there was a man of the Pharisees named Nicodemus, a member of the Jewish ruling council. He came to Jesus at night and said, "Rabbi, we know you are a teacher who has come from God. For no one could perform the miraculous signs you are doing if God were not with him."

In reply Jesus declared, "I tell you the truth, no one can see the kingdom of God unless he is born again,"

"How can a man be born when he is old?" Nicodemus asked. "Surely he cannot enter a second time into his mother's womb to be born!"

Jesus answered, "I tell you the truth, no one can enter the kingdom of God unless he is born of water and the Spirit. Flesh gives birth to flesh, but the Spirit gives birth to spirit. You should not be surprised at my saying, 'You must be born again.' The wind blows wherever it pleases. You hear its sound, but you cannot tell where it comes from or where it is going. So it is with everyone born of the Spirit."

"How can this be?" Nicodemus asked.

"You are Israel's teacher," said Jesus, "and do you not understand these things?"

—John 3:1–10, NIV

An exclusive fraternity, it was. Of the millions in Israel, only six thousand were Pharisees. And Nicodemus was one of the privileged few.

Back in New Testament times, the leaders of Israel were divided between the Pharisees and the Sadducees. Not unlike the Democrats and the Republicans here in the United States, they were at odds with each other most of the time. The Bible also refers to a group called the scribes—those who had chosen the profession of copying and teachers of the law. Some scribes were Pharisees, some Sadducees, and some were from the priesthood.

Nicodemus was a Pharisee. As such, he belonged to a group that paid great attention to detail. Pharisees were careful about pretty much everything—especially the Ten Commandments law, as well as all the other many laws and rules of Israel. However, they also had their laws and special interpretations of God's law.

For instance, a Pharisee could lie to three kinds of people. First of all, he could lie to someone who was lying to him. If somebody was a liar, then you could lie to him. Now that one would give you an open license, wouldn't it? I mean, you could just pretty well use that one any time that you wanted to.

A Pharisee could also lie to a murderer, because it was thought that a life might be saved by lying to a murderer. You could lie to a stranger—a total stranger coming to your land—because he might be wanting to take over your property.

So you could lie to three different kinds of people. You know, that is not unlike some religious groups today. I actually know of a religious group—and I'm not going to name it, but there's one religious group with a name that is sometimes mixed up with ours—and if you're part of that group, you can lie to anyone who isn't, and it's not wrong.

But most of us learn fairly early in life that truth is the best way to go. When I was a kid, I was small, skinny, and weak.

Obviously, since then quite a metamorphosis has taken place, but those who grew up with me know it's true that in my childhood, I was skinny and weak. My older brothers loved to knock me around. My dad too believed firmly in not sparing the rod.

I can remember one time I was in big trouble, and my dad sent my brother out to get the switch. He came back with what looked like a tree to me. I said, "I can't believe you hate me that much."

It's amazing how people used to whip kids like that. You just don't do that anymore these days. I spanked my first three kids. And then I got to Amy, and one day I told her, "Amy, I'm going to have to spank you." She looked at me and said, "Daddy, I know the child abuse number."

Amy did get a spanking. And she really *did* know the number. It's an amazing thing how much the way we bring up our kids has changed. And part of it is that when some kids grow up and become parents, they become convinced there's a better way.

But I remember that as a child, I found out how to keep from getting those whippings: lie! Those whippings made a liar out of me. And later in life, I woke up to the fact that not telling the pure and unadulterated truth—but instead bending it one way or the other—was a trait I had developed and was taking with me through life.

Now, if you're going to be dishonest, you have to have an amazing memory. And I don't have that kind of memory. So now I try to be just as straight and honest as I possibly can be—in addition, your conscience is clear. It is always best to do the right thing. I couldn't remember if I dealt any other way.

As they worked out their theology, the Pharisees, with their typical attention to detail, spelled out just when it was OK to lie and when it wasn't. Because they paid so much attention to the law and how to keep it, Pharisees were considered good men. They weren't homeless drifters or skid-row bums.

Sometimes—and it was true back then and can still be today—

people have decided that the only ones who really need Jesus are the down-and-outers, the people who are at the bottom of the ladder.

I remember when they held a big Billy Graham crusade in New York City years ago. The newspaper complained that the people Billy came to win weren't there—the bums, the drug addicts, the street people. Everybody who came seemed dressed in their best. But being dressed nicely and appearing to be good doesn't mean that we're good.

In 1956, the choice for Outstanding Young Man of America came to a tie—two young men by the first name of Billy. One lived in South Carolina and one lived in Texas. Later, they broke the tie, and the one in Texas won.

The one in South Carolina was Billy Graham. The one in Texas was an up-and-coming businessman named Billy Sol Estes. And he edged out Billy Graham for the award. Billy Sol Estes looked good to a lot of people—and so often, we judge people by how they look.

By 1962, Billy Sol Estes was indicted on fifty-seven counts of fraud and soon was sent to prison. The other Billy went on to top the list of America's most admired men, year after year.

The Pharisees looked good. They kept the law. They were meticulous. They came up with all kinds of rules to be sure they and everyone else stayed "good." A lot of those rules had to do with what was and was not OK to do on the Sabbath. For example, a woman was not to look in the mirror on the Sabbath. Why? Because a woman might see a gray hair and be tempted to pluck it out—and that would be work. Another law the Pharisees made said that if a chicken laid an egg on the Sabbath and nobody ate the egg, everything was fine. But if the chicken laid an egg and somebody ate it, the chicken then had worked to provide a meal and was thus guilty of working on the Sabbath—and had to be killed. Surely, then, if you were a chicken in Israel, you'd have wanted to think twice before laying that Sabbath egg! How ridiculous!

The devil did all he could in Israel—and still does today—to make the Sabbath a burden and hide its beauty. God said simply, "Six days shalt thou labour, and do all thy work: But the seventh day is the sabbath of the LORD thy God" (Exodus 20:9, 10 KJV). But the Pharisees took something God meant to attract His people and used it instead to drive them away.

Along with being meticulous and rule-oriented, Pharisees were also religious. Now, even as a pastor, I want to encourage you to stay as far away from religion as you can! Religion is damaging.

"Look," a man told me one time, "I don't want to have anything to do with religion."

"Neither do I!" I agreed.

"Wait a minute," he said.

"No," I answered, "religion is taking something and making out of it something it is not."

That is religion. I want a spiritual experience. I want an experience with the Lord Jesus Christ. I want to know the way to life. So did Nicodemus, and that's why he came to Jesus at night. He knew something was missing in his spiritual experience—something that should be there.

As noted, in all Israel there were only six thousand Pharisees. And of those six thousand, only seventy were members of the Sanhedrin. And Nicodemus was one of the seventy. The Sanhedrin was like the Senate, and Nicodemus was part of Israel's highest governing body.

I have a painting in my office at home. I don't have too many real paintings that aren't just prints. This is a genuine oil painting created by an outstanding artist. When I first saw it, I immediately wanted it, but it was quite expensive, and I didn't have cash enough to buy it. But fortunately for me, I found that the person who owned it wanted something I had, so we traded, and I have that painting today.

My painting shows Nicodemus with the scrolls of the Scriptures.

In the painting, it's as if he's already been to see Jesus, and later, as he's been reading the book of Isaiah, he sets the scrolls down and is looking into the distance, perhaps thinking about Jesus as the Messiah. To me, it's a beautiful painting, and I really love it.

Nicodemus felt some kind of need in his life, even if he wasn't entirely sure what it was. Now, I don't think that Nicodemus felt that he was any great sinner. He certainly didn't see himself as a down-and-outer. He was too "up" and too "in" to see himself that way. He was on top of things—and he was on the inside. He was not just one of the chosen people.

He was part of the chosen six thousand Pharisees, but even more exclusive, he was part of the chosen seventy of the Sanhedrin. Nicodemus was a ruler. But he was empty. Something inside kept telling him that there surely must be something more.

He wasn't the first to feel that way and won't be the last. How about you? Deep down inside, do you ever feel a vague emptiness? Do you ever wonder if there shouldn't be more to your life? Do you ever sense a need you know is there, but that you can't quite define?

Christ can fill that need, and He's the only One who can. All kinds of religious activity won't do it. Doing good things and not doing bad things won't do it. Being a "good person" won't do it.

Nicodemus perhaps thought that, as He had said to the rich, young ruler, Christ would say to him something such as, "Well, you've done all these good things in Israel, but there's just one thing you lack. And if you will just do this one thing, then you're perfect."

But Christ would come at Nicodemus with a whole different message—and entirely different thought.

Nicodemus, the Bible says, came to Jesus by night. Many people have wondered why. Why did he come by night? In my study, I've discovered that the Pharisees thought the study of the Word and theological things at night had real advantages. A Pharisee was busy all day long, after all. He really did have a lot to do. And then a man like Nicodemus, with added responsibility as a member of the Sanhedrin, was likely busier than most others in Israel. At night he could take a little extra time, with no one pressing him, and study the Word or discuss and debate theological issues with his colleagues.

So Nicodemus may not have come at night, as some say he probably did, because he was ashamed to be seen with Jesus. Any number of other reasons are possible. Perhaps he thought his visit with Jesus might be misunderstood. Or maybe he thought he could have Christ's undivided attention if he waited till nighttime.

Nicodemus may have put some real thought into his opening greeting to Jesus: " 'Rabbi, we know that You are a teacher come from God' " (John 3:2).

The message of John in his Gospel is not that Jesus is a teacher come from God but that Jesus *is* God! Nicodemus was on the way toward Jesus, but he wasn't there yet. He wasn't really a total believer yet. He was looking at it. "I know You've come from God," Nicodemus said, "because a man couldn't do the things You do unless God were with him."

Jesus ignored what Nicodemus said, brushed right past it, looked deep into the Pharisee's heart, and saw there the real questions and concerns of his heart.

" 'Unless one is born again,' " Jesus told him, " 'he cannot see the kingdom of God' " (verse 3).

Clearly, Nicodemus was concerned about being a part of the kingdom. Jesus knew the kingdom was exactly what this great Pharisee was thinking about. He wasn't interested in just keeping the law for the sake of keeping the law. He wasn't interested in all those meticulous things. He was only interested in those things because he thought they pointed the way to salvation—to the kingdom.

Just like you, I want to be a part of the kingdom of God. I

want to be a part of the kingdom of God right here and right now. I also want to be a part of the kingdom of God when Jesus comes in the clouds of glory. But that's still not all. I want to be part of that thousand-year millennial reign in heaven. And finally, I want to be a part of God's kingdom forever and ever and ever.

We sometimes get the idea that a lot of things in this life are important. And maybe some things are. We teach our children that it's important to succeed in life. It's important to do this—or to do that. Yes, those things may be OK—maybe even important. But let's keep our priorities straight. The most important thing in this life is that we seek the kingdom of God and get to know Him and accept what He has done to save us through Jesus.

Jesus cut through all of Nicodemus's well-thought-out remarks and focused in like a laser on what—in his heart of hearts—Nicodemus most wanted to know: the reason he had sought Jesus out under the canopy of the night sky.

Jesus told Nicodemus he needed to be born again.

"How can a man be born when he is old? Can he enter a second time into his mother's womb?" Nicodemus asked, dodging Christ's plain statement.

Now, some say the Pharisee was clueless—that he truly didn't know what Jesus was trying to say. Others would say he was dodging—throwing up a smokescreen, pretending to take Christ's words literally. But maybe Nicodemus was actually entering immediately into the symbolic language. Perhaps he was saying, "I'm getting along in years already. I've already traveled a long way down this Pharisaical road. I've focused years on all this law keeping. How can I turn around now and start some other spiritual experience? How can I go back and start over, like entering my mother's womb again to be born?"

Let's give Nicodemus some credit. He was a Pharisee. He understood this symbolic language Jesus was using. I think he latched on to it immediately and got right into it.

You know, sometimes we start on a path in life, and after a lot of years, we say, "I'm too old now to change. I'm too old to go back. It's too late to start over."

Well, sell that to someone else, because I won't buy it! You're *never* too old! With Jesus, you're never too old to start over. You're never too old to put yourself in His hands. You're never too old to give up on salvation by works—by "being good" and "not being bad." You're never too old to start depending on the Lord Jesus Christ for salvation. You're never too old to start fresh, turn a new page, and completely change the direction of your life. You're never too old to be born again.

The first time in the Bible record where Jesus used the term *born again* is in John, chapter 3. The new birth. Regeneration. Transformation. Conversion. An inner change that takes place.

And this is not a change that takes place by simply saying, "I'm going to change." You know how many times in my lifetime I've said I was going to change? About the same number of times I've said I'm going on a diet! How many times have you said it? Are you going to change just by saying you will? The Bible asks whether a leopard can change his spots or an Ethiopian change the color of his skin. Can they? No! Can I change? Can you? NO!

But Christ says, "I can rebirth you. I can change you if you will allow Me to. I'll bring you forth with newness of life."

When you see someone who's been truly born again, you can't miss the radical change that's happened. You see someone after Christ has reached down into their life and picked them up and changed them, and you can't miss seeing the difference.

I've seen people who have been around Christ and around Christian things all their lives—who know how to talk the talk and walk the walk—people who know how to act exactly pious. And sometimes, I've had people such as these tell me that something special has happened between them and Jesus and how happy they now are. But they really didn't even need to tell me. I could see it. The expressions on their faces told me. Their words told me. Their actions told me. You can't miss a transformed life. For people who experience a new birth, Jesus becomes real.

Some of us were born as babies a long time ago. And some of us later were born in the Lord—again a long time ago. But continuing that experience with Christ means being reborn every day. Born anew. It's as if somehow, the experience I had yesterday is never enough. Our experience of rebirth needs to be fresh every day, never getting old.

"You know," Jesus told Nicodemus, "that which is born of the flesh is flesh, and that which is born of the Spirit is spirit. I say unto you, unless one is born of water and the Spirit, he cannot enter the kingdom of God."

What does that mean? Probably, it has all kinds of different meanings. One of the great things to learn about the Word of God is that when Christ said something, it didn't always just mean one thing. He might have three levels of meaning in something He says. But He means all of them to tell us something.

Someone looks at something Jesus said, and they say, "This is what it says." Well, fine, yes, that *is* what it says. But someone else looks at it, and they say, "No, it says this—it means this." We need to understand that with Christ, it can mean all those things. Unless you are born of water and the Spirit—some say that refers to water baptism. That's fine—nothing wrong with that. I'll accept that—no problem whatsoever. But can it also mean something else?

Others say Jesus was talking about natural birth. After all, we all know that an unborn child is wrapped and enveloped in water.

Then we think of something else. Christ speaks of the Word of God as the water of life. So can we ever be born again if the water of the Word isn't somehow involved?

If you're hungering and thirsting after righteousness, you go to the Word to be filled. And I don't care what version you go to. I'm personally happy for some of those versions.

I found a long time ago that if I had trouble sleeping at night, all I had to do was pick up the King James Version of the Bible and begin reading it. I guess the devil put me to sleep, because I'd go right to sleep. Do you ever have any trouble sleeping, and you pick up a King James Version and begin to read it, and before long all the "thee's" and "thou's" and "shouldest's" and "couldest's" have you out like a light? Now, don't get me wrong—the King James is still my favorite version.

I recommend some of the more contemporary translations—even some of the paraphrases—for devotional reading. Some of them may not be the best for deep theological study, but sometimes a fresh rendition of familiar Bible passages can open new insights.

And of course, I recommend the Gospel of John as the best place to start. Maybe for a long time, you've told yourself that one of these days, you're going to get serious about daily Bible reading. So why not start this today? Tell yourself that you won't listen to any of your own excuses any longer. Make up your mind to read a chapter a day—or at least five verses a day—but as the Nike shoe slogan says, "Just do it!"

I once had a business that I later sold, but for years at that business, all of us had worship together every morning—unless snow kept us from coming in. We had about twenty-five or thirty employees, and we'd read a page of the Bible each morning. Through the thirteen years I had that business, we read the Bible through several times. We marked each time we had read it through, and we were just reading one page a day.

So again, let me urge you to start now, start with a newer translation, and start with the Gospel of John. Read it through, then go to a book outside the four Gospels and read it through. Then return and pick up one of the other four Gospels. Keep alternating till you've finished all four Gospels and four other books—then, keep going!

Keep the Word of God alive in your heart. I've personally

found the book of Proverbs a wonderful help in my own walk with God. It has thirty-one chapters, just as many months have thirty-one days—a good daily match. In fact, you might want to read a chapter of Proverbs every day, no matter what other Bible book you're working through. It contains beautiful, vital, and practical counsel on how to live.

We must become people of the Book again. So many of us are reading everything except what God has told us to read—His Word. Read it, and if you don't understand something, don't stay there long—don't get bogged down. Put a check mark by it and look it up later—but keep moving in the Word of God.

I am quite sure that when Jesus met Nicodemus, Jesus gave him life. Jesus filled his emptiness. Jesus answered his deepest longings.

" 'You should not be surprised at my saying, "You must be born again." The wind blows wherever it pleases. You hear its sound, but you cannot tell where it comes from or where it is going. So it is with everyone born of the Spirit.'

" 'How can this be?' Nicodemus asked.

" 'You are Israel's teacher,' said Jesus, 'and do you not understand these things?' " (verses 7–10, NIV).

You—a member of the Sanhedrin, a Pharisee, a teacher—are teaching the people, and you don't know these things? No wonder those people missed knowing Christ. Until that night meeting, even their teacher was not ready for Him.

Jesus didn't have fifty thousand people in a stadium listening to Him preach. He had one man—one on one, the greatest sermon in all of Scripture—and Jesus preached it to a one-man audience. That's exactly how salvation comes—to one man at a time, one woman, one child. It's always one on one. It's Christ in you. Salvation doesn't come to one church at a time. So it doesn't work to try and be saved by belonging to a church. Salvation doesn't come to one family at a time. So it doesn't work to try and be saved by belonging to a family. The only family to make it to the kingdom is the family of God—and every member of that family is saved one at a time.

Hyde Park in London has an area called the Speakers' Corner, where people can get up on a soapbox—and they've actually got some old crates and soapboxes around there—and can speak on any subject. When I visited there once, I couldn't help but drift over and listen to some of these "great philosophers" as they expounded. It's quite an atmosphere, people arguing back and forth with the various speakers.

Years ago—according to H. M. S. Richards Sr., in his book *Feed My Sheep,* a man was preaching the gospel there, and skeptics were ribbing him and shouting out to him. One of them tried to get the preacher into an argument, but the preacher ignored him. So the heckler turned his attention to a young man assisting the speaker, who was carrying some pamphlets.

"What do you know about Christianity anyway?" the heckler asked.

"Not much," the young man answered.

"Well," he continued, "then tell me, when was Christ born? What was the date of the birth of Christ?"

"I don't know."

"And where was Christ born?"

"I don't know."

"When did He die? What was the date of His death?"

"I don't know."

The skeptic looked at him and smirked.

"You don't know very much about Him, do you?"

"No, sir," the young man replied, "I don't know a lot of these things you're talking about. But I know this: I know that six months ago, my life was miserable. I came to this park because I was at the end of my rope. I drank up every single thing I made. My wife was miserable. She cried as she went about her work during the day. When I came home at night, I'd be drunk, and the children were afraid of me. They would run and hide under the bed, because they were afraid I would beat them. I was miserable. I couldn't keep a job. One night I came through this park, and I was thinking of taking my life."

The young man gestured toward a park bench and continued. "I sat on that bench right over there, and I began to hear this man preach, and he was talking about Jesus and how Jesus could save and how Jesus could change your life, and I was at the end of my rope. I got up, and I walked over there, and I stood right there and gave my life to Jesus Christ. Now things are different in my life. I've held a steady job now for six months. I take home every dime I make to buy the food and clothing and pay the rent. My wife is happy—she sings as she goes about her work. When I come home in the afternoon, my children run out the front door and through the gate and jump into my arms. They hug me and kiss me and they say, 'Daddy's come home!' "

The young man looked the heckler straight in the eye. "I don't know all those things you're talking about, but I do know what Jesus did for me!"

The heckler was silenced—no one can argue with a testimony. What about you? What is your testimony? Has Jesus done this for and in you? He can, and He will, if you will let Him. How about doing that right now, right where you are? And then at the bottom of this page, write the date and time of your new birth with Jesus—just as your birth certificate has the time and date you were born physically!

If you asked Jesus into your heart right now, you are a new creation, you have been born again. And this birth will last forever!

The Woman at the Well

Jesus was so well accepted around Jerusalem that the negative attention of the Pharisees—which till now had been focused on John the Baptist—was now turned upon Him. Not yet ready for the confrontation He knew was coming, He chose to return to Galilee.

Now, the best route to Galilee today was the best route then, as well—from Jerusalem to Jericho, on the Jericho road ("where there's room for just two," as the old song goes), then along the Jordan Valley on a very flat road that follows the Jordan River, right up to the Sea of Galilee. This route was taken by most travelers from Jerusalem going north. This was even the route the good Samaritan traveled, when he found and helped the man along the way who had been attacked by thieves.

But Jesus didn't take this route on this particular trip, even though it was the best and most direct way to go. Verse 4 of John 4 says, "He needed to go through Samaria." Jesus went that way because He had a divine appointment with a woman at Jacob's Well.

For a religious Jew to go through Samaria was extremely unusual. The Jews had nothing to do with the Samaritans. They despised them so much that they would not even allow the shadow of a Samaritan to fall on them. Can you imagine how much fun a Samaritan with a sense of humor could have had with his shadow, in a crowd of religious Jewish people?

These hard feelings started during the last years of the reign of Solomon. Known as the great builder, Solomon not only built the great temple but also many other great projects. For these projects, he not only collected taxes but also demanded that each citizen work so many weeks out of the year on the projects without pay! This was especially difficult for those who lived in the north of Israel. Making it even more burdensome, the projects were mostly in the Jerusalem area, so this meant they had to travel to Jerusalem and spend time away from their homes.

Resentment had built to a crescendo by the time Solomon died, and as the kingdom was being passed to his son Rehoboam, the tribes from the north saw an opportunity to make their move and see if things could be changed. Jeroboam was chosen to represent them, and he approached Rehoboam and told him that the people were fed up with the forced labor and the heavy yoke, and Jeroboam asked the new king if he would be willing to ease up, with the assurance that if he did, the people would serve him. Rehoboam asked for three days to think about it (see 1 Kings 12:1–24).

The old men who had advised his father told him to ease up. Interesting, isn't it, that Solomon—the wisest man who ever lived—had advisors! True wisdom seeks counsel, listens to the ideas of others, and gleans that which is best! Only a fool thinks he knows it all and refuses to seek advice.

Rehoboam should have taken their advice, but he decided to get a second opinion. This time, he went to the young men who were his friends, who had grown up with him, and no doubt were going to be a part of his administration. To paraphrase them, they said, "Tell them, 'You ain't seen nothing yet!' " (see 1 Kings 12:10, 11).

When Rehoboam took this advice and shared that information, the northern tribes rebelled, killed Adoniram—who was in charge of forced labor—and Rehoboam had to run back to Jerusalem with his "tail between his legs." As a result, the northern area began as a separate kingdom with Jeroboam chosen as king. The new northern kingdom now had ten of the twelve tribes, and Rehoboam ended up with only the tribes of Judah and Benjamin.

To his credit, Rehoboam took the blame for the split (see 1 Kings 12:24) and refused to attack the north, when God sent the word through His prophet that he shouldn't fight his brothers.

The tension really increased after Assyria attacked the northern kingdom in 720 B.C. and forced intermarriage. To the Jews in the south, who had been miraculously delivered from the Assyrian army of Sennacherib, this was even more reason for them to resent the "half-breeds"—who became known as Samaritans. Then, when Judah was conquered by the Babylonians and taken into a seventy-year captivity, they dreamed of returning to their homeland. When that prayer was answered in 457 B.C., they determined to rebuild Jerusalem, which was in ruins.

While Nehemiah was rebuilding the wall, Sanballat and Tobiah, in the north, offered to come and help. The offer was rejected, and the Samaritans saw that even after the Babylonian captivity of the southern kingdom, they were not welcome in Jerusalem. As a result, they built a temple on Mount Gerizim, called that their "holy mountain," and the animosity continued to grow. So you can see why it was unusual that a group of Jews would go through Samaria.

But the Bible says that "Jesus needed to go through Samaria." Before the Hubble Space Telescope, it was thought that there were as many as sixty-five thousand galaxies in the universe. That number was later increased to one hundred thousand, and then to two hundred fifty thousand galaxies. After Hubble, we are now told that there are innumerable galaxies! If only one planet in each galaxy is inhabited, the population of the universe would be something we might never calculate. But one woman on just one tiny planet in one of those countless galaxies—and a Samaritan woman at that—needs Jesus, and He goes out of His way to meet her at Jacob's Well, located at Sychar, right in the heart of Samaria!

Why? Not because this woman was good—she quite definitely was *not* good. We love those who are good, beautiful, talented, or successful. But I've concluded that God's love is an expression of His character and doesn't depend on the worthiness of the object of that love.

Remember when Joseph Bates went into Battle Creek, Michigan, during the early years of the Adventist movement and inquired of the postmaster to find "the most honest man in town"? He was directed to a man named David Hewitt. If someone had asked the same question in Sychar, they would emphatically *not* have been directed to the woman Jesus met at the well. Neither was she known as the most virtuous! But you see, God loves us, even when we are not perfect!

Now, the Bible says it was about the "sixth hour" (John 4:6). Much discussion has taken place about when this actually was. Using Jewish time, it would have been noon. Calculating with Roman time, it would have been six o'clock in the evening. Roman time was normally used, and Alfred Edersheim, in his great work *The Life and Times of Jesus the Messiah,* argues for this being 6:00 P.M.—the end of the day. However, I stand with Ellen G. White, who says that it was noon. And to me, this would seem even more of a miracle—that Jesus and the woman would be at the well at noon, rather than at the end of the day.

Why? Sychar was about a day's walk from Jerusalem. Normally, the evening meal would be the big meal of the day, when one was traveling. A portion would be saved for breakfast, then what was left—usually not much—would be placed in a pouch to be eaten at noon, and the process would start all over again in the evening. The Bible says that the disciples had gone into town to purchase food—unusual for them to do in the middle of the day. But for some reason, we are not told why, they had gone into town. Perhaps they had left Jerusalem unexpectedly in the middle of the day before—then arrived at Sychar at noon the next day, instead of at the end of a day's walk.

So why was the woman there at noon? This was not a normal time to draw water. Normally, this would happen in the early morning or late in the day, not in the middle or heat of the day. I've heard preachers expound on a supposition that she went there when she did to avoid the other women who came there, because of their criticism of her lifestyle. But I doubt this explanation. This was not a shy woman—she even talks back to Jesus and later goes to town to call the people out to hear Him. I believe she was more than able to stand up to the wagging tongues of the local gossips. She perhaps knew as much dirt on them as they did on her, and if not on them, then at least on their husbands!

I think if we could ask her why, she would say, "I don't know why. I was totally out of water, so I just had to go to the well!" But if we asked Jesus, He would tell us that she had a divine appointment with Him that she didn't know about!

Now the Bible says that Jesus was "tired."

"Wait just a minute," you say. "We have learned in John 1 that Jesus is God, the Creator—that He has always existed and never gets tired."

Yes, but He is also human and has two natures! And His human nature was tired.

A woman in southern Oregon came to me after a meeting one night and asked me about the nature of Christ. I told her what I believe the Bible teaches—that Jesus is 100 percent human and 100 percent divine. But, she asked, "Did Jesus have Adam's nature before the Fall—or after the Fall?" In other words, did Jesus have any special advantage over us?

First of all, let me say that I believe that no one was ever tempted more than Jesus was. The devil knew that it was all riding on Jesus, and you can be assured he did everything he could to cause Him to fall, going far beyond the account that we have of the temptation on the mountain. Yet Jesus did not sin. Had Jesus had any special benefits not available to us, the devil would have cried "foul"!

But instead of trying to answer her question, I took a page out of Jesus' book and asked her a question.

"What good did Adam's nature before the Fall do him? Did it keep him from falling? How about the one-third of the angels of heaven? They each had a perfect nature, but did that keep them from falling?"

We know that Christ's life was perfect and that His perfect life is accepted by God in place of our imperfect lives.

Yes, Jesus was tired, but not too tired to talk to this woman about eternal life. The amazing thing, in that culture, is that He would talk to a woman at all—especially a Samaritan. Men didn't speak to women, especially a religious Jew to a Samaritan woman! In fact, one group of Pharisees actually went so far as to wear blinders—such as race horses do—so they weren't even able to see a woman! They often bumped into things with their limited range of vision, so their critics called them "the bruised and bleeding Pharisees."

Had Jesus not been a Jew, the woman would normally have offered Him a drink of water—as a polite thing to do—from the large gourd she used as a bucket. When she didn't, Jesus asked her for a drink, and this surprised her. She questioned why He, a Jew, would ask her, a Samaritan woman, for a drink, as she saw the uniqueness of the moment. The dialogue here is so remarkable that if you don't remember it in total, turn to John 4 and read it for yourself.

Jesus offers her the "Water of Life"—which is Himself and His gift of life eternal. She misses the point at first, and then He says to her, "Go call your husband." She tells Him that she has no husband, and He tells her that she has spoken truthfully—that she has had five husbands and hasn't even bothered to marry the last fellow, with whom she is living in sin! She wasn't much good at interpersonal relationships!

How could she be a worse sinner? Yet Jesus, knowing the worst about her, still reached out to her with the offer of eternal life. When we met Nicodemus in an earlier chapter, we met a good man—a religious Jew who still needed to be born again to be saved. Now, we meet a sinful Samaritan woman who also needs to be born again.

Yes, Jesus knows all about us, yet He still meets us at the well of life and offers that water that will quench our thirst. For some people, you will never be good enough to satisfy them, but Jesus meets you where you are. He's not going to leave you where you are, though. If you let Him, He will lead—not drive, but lead—you along the road to a life of relationship with Him and obedience in Him.

You see, God is still saving the lost! When we see hard-core sinners, we tend to shy away from witnessing to them. We look instead for those who do not smoke, drink, or live immorally, and we think, *All I have to do is convince them to change a few of their doctrinal beliefs—don't even have to clean them up—and they will make good Adventists.*

The man next door to you may have a burnt offering of pig out on the grill, a can of beer in his hand, and a stinky cigar that his wife won't even let him smoke in the house—and all those aromas drift over and cause you to close your windows. Perhaps too often, we tend to avoid this type. But at those times when I've gone over and initiated contact, I have found a true soul worth saving underneath that exterior. Jesus saw beneath the outer conduct of the woman at the well and knew that here was a person with a longing only He could satisfy.

Some time ago church members John Taylor and Dexter LeBlanc became acquainted with a couple in south Louisiana, who were fully involved in a common New Orleans lifestyle. Smoking, drinking—you name it!

One Saturday night, John and Dexter began studying the Bible with this couple. They had no idea that these worldly people had an interest in Scripture. One by one, they covered our fundamental beliefs. By morning, the neighbors had quit smoking, drinking, eating unclean foods (a really big thing in south Louisiana with all the gumbo and such), had accepted the Sabbath and all the truths we hold so dear, and had given their hearts fully to Jesus Christ—all in one night!

When I met the lady years later (her husband had died in the faith), she was an officer of her church. She was now such a beautiful, born-again Christian that I couldn't even imagine she had ever lived the lifestyle she once did.

This is exactly what happened to the woman at the well. "The woman said to Him, 'I know that Messiah is coming (He who is called Christ); when that One comes, He will declare all things to us.' Jesus said to her, 'I who speak to you am He' " (John 4:25, 26, NASB).

The Samaritan woman accepted Jesus at that very moment and went to get her friends. As a result, the Bible tells us, "Many of the Samaritans from that town believed in him" (verse 39, NIV). And they urged Him to stay—so He stayed for two days and taught them, and even more of them accepted Him.

When God touches your life in a powerful way, you cannot help but be a witness! That leaves just two questions: What has Jesus done for you? and, Have you shared it lately with anyone?

Every day, God sets up divine appointments for you and me—opportunities to share what He has done for us. But whether those chances are seized on or passed by—that is up to us!

HEALING THE IMPOTENT MAN

Some time later, Jesus went up to Jerusalem for a feast of the Jews. Now there is in Jerusalem near the Sheep Gate a pool, which in Aramaic is called Bethesda and which is surrounded by five covered colonnades. Here a great number of disabled people used to lie—the blind, the lame, the paralyzed. One who was there had been an invalid for thirty-eight years. When Jesus saw him lying there and learned that he had been in this condition for a long time, he asked him, "Do you want to get well?"

"Sir," the invalid replied, "I have no one to help me into the pool when the water is stirred. While I am trying to get in, someone else goes down ahead of me."

Then Jesus said to him, "Get up! Pick up your mat and walk." At once the man was cured; he picked up his mat and walked.

The day on which this took place was a Sabbath, and so the Jews said to the man who had been healed, "It is the Sabbath; the law forbids you to carry your mat."

But he replied, "The man who made me well said to me, 'Pick up your mat and walk.'"

So they asked him, "Who is this fellow who told you to pick it up and walk?"

The man who was healed had no idea who it was, for Jesus had slipped away into the crowd that was there.

Later Jesus found him at the temple and said to him, "See, you are well again. Stop sinning or something worse may happen to you." The man went away and told the Jews that it was Jesus who had made him well.

So, because Jesus was doing these things on the Sabbath, the Jews persecuted him.

—John 5:1–16, NIV

If you were a Jew living within fifteen miles of Jerusalem back in the time of Jesus, you were obliged to attend two of the major religious feasts each year: the Feast of Tabernacles and Passover.

But many came from much greater distances. Jesus, John says, made His way to one of these feasts—though John doesn't say which one. But when Jesus arrived, He walked to the pool near the Sheep Gate—today known as Saint Stephen's Gate, since it's near the place where Stephen was stoned.

Near the Sheep Gate, John wrote, was a pool—the pool of Bethesda. For years skeptics said no such pool ever existed in Jerusalem. But archeologists found a pool that fits the Bible description of it exactly. I personally am convinced the site they uncovered is indeed the place where Jesus performed the miracle John described in his fifth chapter.

Now, it seems that the first part of this story—the part about the angel coming down to move the waters—was not in the oldest copies of John's Gospel that we have. The earlier ones don't mention it at all. So that part of the story may well have been added later.

Somehow, though, the people who waited around the pool for healing believed that once the water moved, the first one in would be healed. Now, we know that isn't how Jesus heals. He didn't heal people on the basis of who was fast enough to be the first one in the pool. After all, the person who was most ill and in the greatest need of healing might be the very one who was least able to get into the pool quickly.

John says Jesus saw a man at the pool who had been sick for

thirty-eight years. We don't know exactly how long he had been at this spot hoping to be healed, but he never seemed able to get into the pool fast enough.

So Jesus came along and said to him, "Sir, do you want to be made whole? Do you want to be made well?"

Sometimes people are sick, but they really don't want to get well. Maybe they're getting too much good attention from staying sick. But this man really wanted to be healed. I believe this man had been crying out for help all those years. And I believe Jesus had him earmarked for healing even before He left heaven and came to earth.

So the day came—and Jesus and the man met at the pool: a divine appointment!

Jesus said to him, " 'Rise' "! In the Greek language of that day, it was a command. Then Jesus followed with two more commands: " 'take up your bed and walk' " (John 5:8).

And the man obeyed, and in that exact order. The man immediately stood to his feet. He reached down and took up his bed. Then he began walking along the poolside.

When I was a boy, I wondered how on earth the man could pick up his bed! I mean, my bed had four posts, a frame, some springs, a mattress. How could this man carry his bed around? But of course, this man's bed wasn't at all like mine. It was just a little pallet—something he could probably just roll up and carry under his arm.

When the man heard Jesus' commands, he could have said, "Wait a minute, Lord. Let me take a few steps first and see if this walking thing really happens. If it does, then I'll come back and get my bed."

No, the man believed. He stood. He picked up his bed. And he walked.

Jesus healed this man for more than one reason. Of course, He wanted to relieve this man's suffering and honor his faith. But He also wanted to bring about a confrontation with the

Jews, so He could teach them—and everyone listening in—some great truths.

From the pool, the man went to the temple, no doubt walking around with his bed still under his arm. The Jews immediately saw him. Now their laws about the Sabbath commandment had become so ridiculous that, for example, if you even had a needle stuck inside your lapel, you were carrying a load. You'd be breaking the Sabbath and were subject to being stoned. So if someone with a needle in their lapel could be stoned, you can imagine the danger this man was in for carrying his bed around.

Jesus was the Creator of the Sabbath. And He said that the Sabbath was made for man—not man for the Sabbath. God didn't make a Sabbath and surround it with endless rules, and then create human beings so they could keep all these laws. God never intended to create human beings to live as slaves to gazillions of Sabbath rules—He didn't make man for the Sabbath.

No, He created the Sabbath as a priceless gift for man! The Sabbath was for man—not man for the Sabbath. But the Jewish leaders got it all turned around. Maybe God didn't attach hundreds of rules to the Sabbath—but they certainly did! And by the time Jesus came, the Sabbath He had created as a blessing and a gift for men and women had become one of their heaviest burdens.

But sadly enough, it wasn't just God's people in Bible times who did this. It still happens today. As a child, I used to dread the arrival of the Sabbath. And I know I wasn't the only one. I dreaded seeing the sun go down on Friday. I wanted it to stay up just a little longer so I could enjoy life a little more—because once that big round sun disappeared, so did all the fun and joy in life, at least that's how it seemed to me.

In our own way, today some of us have done exactly what the people in Jesus' day did—we've piled on so many rules about Sabbath keeping, so many "don't do its"—that we end up dreading the Sabbath. And in doing that, we've missed out on the whole idea of what Jesus was trying to accomplish by giving us the Sabbath. Because the Sabbath isn't about what we *can't do*—it's a day when we *get to* do a lot of awesome things!

That's why Jesus changed the Sabbath.

Yes, when Jesus came, He changed the Sabbath. But not from Saturday to Sunday. Instead, He changed it from a day of burdensome "don'ts" to a day of delight—spiritually, physically, socially—in every way. And if you are continuing to keep the Sabbath the way the Old Testament Jews did, friend, you've changed it back from the way Jesus changed it. Because He said it is lawful to do good on the Sabbath.

Now listen, they could have picked up stones and killed that man for carrying his bed. If they had really wanted to, they could have done it even on the Sabbath—and by their rules, that would not have been profaning the Sabbath. What did Jesus say to them?

> But Jesus answered them, "My Father has been working until now, and I have been working."
>
> Therefore the Jews sought all the more to kill Him, because He not only broke the Sabbath, but also said that God was His Father, making Himself equal with God. Then Jesus answered and said to them, "Most assuredly, I say to you, the Son can do nothing of Himself, but what He sees the Father do; for whatever He does, the Son also does in like manner. For the Father loves the Son, and shows Him all things that He Himself does; and He will show Him greater works than these, that you may marvel. For as the Father raises the dead and gives life to them, even so the Son gives life to whom He will. For the Father judges no one, but has committed all judgment to the Son, that all should honor the Son just as they honor the Father. He who does not honor the Son does not honor the Father who sent Him" (verses 17–23).

You see, in their scheme of things, they had come to the place where they honestly thought it would be better to kill on the Sabbath than to give life on the Sabbath—to help on the Sabbath, to do something positive and good on the Sabbath. And they had built into the law of God all of their own restraints, and today, let us be careful that we don't do the same.

Now don't misunderstand me. I don't believe we should ever make God's day a day of merchandise, a day of work, a day of sport. I'm not saying that at all. I'm saying, though, that it is still lawful to do good on the Sabbath. Instead of being so ready to make a whole long list of those *don'ts* for the Sabbath, we need to be making a list of *dos* for the Sabbath—spiritually exciting things we can do that are great and fun and invigorating for our kids, our young people, but things that are different from the things that they do all the other six days.

When Christ came, to be very honest with you, He talked far differently about the Sabbath than the way even Moses talked about it. But we need to remember that this is the Lawgiver. This is Jesus. This is the Creator. If anybody knows how the Sabbath should be kept, He knows.

So you don't have to question what He is saying. He's giving the Sabbath a new dimension. In Moses' day, they couldn't even leave their tents. Now, that was a special situation, and we know that. Here God had brought all these people out of Egypt, and they had drifted away from God completely. They needed some training, and He couldn't control that bunch out there, so the easiest thing to do was to say, "Stay in your tent."

Moses never had the insight into the Sabbath and its meaning that Jesus had. Jesus, the Great Lawgiver, was making a change, and they couldn't accept it. Those Jews looked at Him, and they began to say, "We're going to kill Him." They didn't accept His authority to be making changes to their system of religion—to their way of keeping the Sabbath.

Some people come along today and say, "Well, Jesus was a good teacher—a wonderful teacher, a good man, a great person, a real example, a human being who was a 'cut above'—and all of this kind of baloney."

Listen, you can't believe that, if you believe Christ. Because Jesus said that He was God. Your read this to some of the more liberal Christians today, and they will say, "Oh, no—that's not really what He was saying."

Yes, that's *exactly* what He was saying! The Jews understood what He was saying too. " 'My Father is always at his work to this very day, and I, too, am working' " (John 5:17, NIV). You see, God rested the first Sabbath, yes. But He didn't rest because He was tired from His labor. God doesn't get tired. That's not His quality—that's your quality, and that's my quality.

We all get exhausted sometimes. And I don't want to do away with the Sabbath. Please, don't *ever* do away with the Sabbath! I really worry about people who don't have a Sabbath, don't you? Believe me, I do, because they don't have that time to really rest at least once a week—and I believe in that rest. Some of you work really hard during the week, and you are so emotionally whipped by the time the Sabbath hours come that you *need* that special rest. So don't ever let somebody condemn you for taking a little rest on the Sabbath—you need it. If you are tired, that's one reason God made the Sabbath and gave it to us. I think one of the greatest experiences of all time is the Sabbath afternoon nap. You sure don't get one of those any *other* day of the week, do you? I don't—and I doubt if you do either.

Now, here in John, we are finding that Jesus claims equality with God. And Jesus says, " 'My Father has been working until now, and I have been working' " (verse 17). You see, when God rested at Creation, He was resting from His finished work of creation. But if God ever totally rested, the whole universe would be out of line, wouldn't it? God never really, honestly rested in the way you and I rest.

Here, Christ is saying, "I don't rest either. Because I am God."

And this was more than the Jewish leaders could take. "For this reason the Jews tried all the harder to kill him; not only was he breaking the Sabbath, but he was even calling God his own Father, making himself equal with God" (verse 18, NIV).

And He did. And He is. And that's the message of John, my friend. Right from the beginning of the book, as we've said over and over, the message of John is this: *He is God! Jesus Christ is God!* He's not simply a good man. He's not just a prophet. He's not a teacher only. But even though He was all of those things, *He is God.* The Son of God is verily God.

Now that's a message. Some of you reading along have entered into that critical point of life called middle age—the most dangerous time of life ever. It makes even the teenage years pale by comparison. This is a time when you've started to think and wonder and question. And you've looked at the whole scheme of things and thought to yourself, *Who am I kidding? I don't even know if I believe or not.*

You see, that's the great danger of middle age—you begin to question. Let me tell you what you have to do at that point. I can tell you from experience what you have to do. You go back to the basics. Go back and take a look at God. You take at look at Jesus Christ, and you make up your mind whether you believe in Him and whether you believe that He is exactly who He says He is. Because there is no middle ground with Jesus. He's either who He says He is, or He's the worst blasphemer ever—no middle ground, my friend. You've got to make up your mind about Jesus. And when you make up your mind about Jesus, you make up your mind about God, because you can't believe in One without believing in the Other.

Sometimes people say, "Well, look, can't I believe in God and maybe not believe in Jesus?" NO—you can't! Because the Father testified of Jesus, and vice versa. You can't believe in God and not believe in Jesus. You just can't do it. " 'This is My beloved Son,' " the Father said, " 'in whom I am well pleased' " (Matthew 3:17).

Over and over the Scriptures testify of Christ, that He is who He claims to be. You see His person, His quality, and His works. " 'Most assuredly, I say to you, the Son can do nothing of Himself, but what He sees the Father do; for whatever He does, the Son also does in like manner' " (John 5:19).

Sometimes people have taken that text and tried to say that it means Christ is not equal to God—that He is *under* God. Oh, no. What that means is that God and His Son are totally in concert together. What Jesus was doing on this earth, He was not doing *out of harmony* with God, He was doing it *in harmony* with God.

Sometimes folks will knock on your door. Have you ever had them knock on your door? You know, the ones who have come to "witness" to you?

And they'll read that text to you and say, "Now, in the Greek that text says . . ." And that's supposed to really influence and impress you. But try to get them to read the Greek a few texts further on. Trouble is, they know the Greek on just that one text.

I've had some fun when they come by. I say, "Oh, you know Greek?" And they will always say something like, "Yes, we know a little Greek."

"Wonderful!" I'll say. "I know a little Greek myself. I took four years of Greek. So let's look at some more Greek here. Let's get the Greek New Testament out, and let's look at that."

And they just can't go beyond those one or two texts somebody has fed them some information about. It's funny how all of a sudden they don't have an argument anymore. I'm not trying to put them on the spot, but, friend, anybody who comes along and tells you that Jesus is somehow less than *fully God* is a heretic. Anybody who tells you that is from a cult—a sect. I don't care who they are.

Jesus is fully God—not any kind of lesser God. He is God in a man's body. You know, maybe sometimes we look around at this messed-up world and are tempted to say, "God, why don't You come down here and see how it really is?"

But then we instantly know that He did exactly that—He came down here and saw how it really is. We don't ever have to question that our God knows what we're up against, because Jesus does know. Look again at John 5:20, " 'For the Father loves the Son, and shows Him all things that He Himself does; and He will show Him greater works than these.' "

Then read on from verses 21 through 24, " 'For as the Father raises the dead and gives life to them, even so the Son gives life to whom He will. For the Father judges no one, but has committed all judgment to the Son, that all should honor the Son just as they honor the Father. He who does not honor the Son does not honor the Father who sent Him. Most assuredly, I say to you, he who hears My word and believes in Him who sent Me has everlasting life, and shall not come into judgment, but has passed from death into life.' "

There's the secret of it all. If you believe in Him, you trust Him. If you accept Him as your Savior and as the God of all gods, then, He says, you've passed from death into life. That is righteousness by faith, my friend—that is it. You can take righteousness by faith and dissect it in a jillion different ways and make it all scientific.

An amazing thing is that some who study or teach about righteousness by faith want you to say back to them exactly what they've said to you about it. I took some classes at the Seminary from one of the great proponents of righteousness by faith, and he would ask us to write a paragraph on a test. And if we didn't write it back to him verbatim, word for word, just as he had said it, then he told us we didn't understand it.

So many times, that's the way we are. We think we are the only ones who can describe righteousness by faith. But it's not describing it that's important, because righteousness by faith is *an experience*. It's trusting in Jesus Christ to change you—and that's the whole story of this man here in John, who could not help himself. He couldn't even get to the pool. He was sick—

and he couldn't heal himself. He couldn't even get to the place where superstition taught him that there was a *place* for healing.

You know, that is our state too. Christ has to come and do for us, and change us, and take us from death to life—and that's what He did, and that's what He does. You see, this miracle of healing in John was a miracle of creation. I don't know what was wrong with this man, but he had some real problems with his physical body that could not be healed. But Jesus just made them new. Christ just spoke, and they were made new, right then and there.

As we look at these miracles Jesus performed—for example, the miracle at Cana, when Jesus turned the water into wine—we realize something important. Christ needed absolutely nothing to do those miracles. At Cana, He had no grapes when He turned the water to wine. All He had was just water. No grapes. No vines. Just suddenly, He created wine from water. Creative power! And that creative power demonstrated that Jesus was God.

John's book was written between A.D. 90 and A.D. 100. These events took place between A.D. 31 and 32. John's now an old man. He's held all of these things in his mind all of these years. He's thought a lot about them.

There's all kind of theology going around these days. The apostle Paul's writings are fabulous. But let me tell you, if you do not understand and read Paul in line with Matthew, Mark, Luke, and John, you will misunderstand the apostle Paul. If you were to read him simply without having their background, you would misunderstand. Why? Because Paul is presupposing you understand what Matthew, Mark, Luke, and John are saying. He's speaking to specific problems. When you study these books together, you can see exactly what the apostle Paul is saying.

But now John as an old man sees people starting to think, *Well, maybe Christ was just a good man.* And John says, "No. I have to take the message to the people. Not just another story of Jesus, but a different book—a book that points out that Jesus is

God." So John gives all these proofs of Christ's divinity.

Notice now, as we continue in chapter 5, what John wrote about the two resurrections: " 'Most assuredly, I say to you, the hour is coming, and now is, when the dead will hear the voice of the Son of God; and those who hear will live' " (verse 25).

Now, two resurrections are spoken of here, and this first one is the spiritual resurrection. I believe this. Look at this: " 'For as the Father has life in Himself, so He has granted the Son to have life in Himself, and has given Him authority to execute judgment also, because He is the Son of Man. Do not marvel at this; for the hour is coming in which all who are in the graves will hear His voice and come forth—those who have done good, to the resurrection of life, and those who have done evil, to the resurrection of condemnation.' " (verses 26–29).

So actually, we see three resurrections. The first is the spiritual resurrection. That man down at the pool was dead, for all practical purposes. Spiritually, he didn't even know who Jesus was. When he received Him, suddenly, he had a whole new life. Perhaps we're cruising along, and we're spiritually dead. We have no life in us. The Spirit of God comes to us. Christ comes to us. We accept Him, and we're changed. We've come to a newness of life—a spiritual resurrection. Christ came to the Jews, and many of them were dead—they were spiritually dead. You see, the Bible tells us that "the letter killeth, but the spirit giveth life" (2 Corinthians 3:6, KJV). They were so hung up on the letter, that they were dead. But Jesus came to them, saying, "I want to give you life. The Spirit gives life."

Let's "bite off" another good long piece of John 5 now and take a look at it.

> "I can of Myself do nothing. As I hear, I judge; and My judgment is righteous, because I do not seek My own will but the will of the Father who sent Me. If I bear witness of Myself, My witness is not true. There is another who

bears witness of Me, and I know that the witness which He witnesses of Me is true. You have sent to John, and he has borne witness to the truth. Yet I do not receive testimony from man, but I say these things that you may be saved. He was the burning and shining lamp, and you were willing for a time to rejoice in his light. But I have a greater witness than John's; for the works which the Father has given Me to finish—the very works that I do—bear witness of Me, that the Father has sent Me. And the Father Himself, who sent Me, has testified of Me. You have neither heard His voice at any time, nor seen His form. But you do not have His word abiding in you, because whom He sent, Him you do not believe. You search the Scriptures, for in them you think you have eternal life; and these are they which testify of Me. But you are not willing to come to Me that you may have life. I do not receive honor from men. But I know you, that you do not have the love of God in you. I have come in My Father's name, and you do not receive Me; if another comes in his own name, him you will receive. How can you believe, who receive honor from one another, and do not seek the honor that comes from the only God? Do not think that I shall accuse you to the Father; there is one who accuses you—Moses, in whom you trust. For if you believed Moses, you would believe Me; for he wrote about Me. But if you do not believe his writings, how will you believe My words?" (verses 30–47).

This great message, going down through verse 47, is one of the great sermons Christ delivered on His own divinity—and on His own mission. He says, "Believe, and you will pass from death unto life." Let me tell you something, if anybody knows we are imperfect, it is God. If anybody knows we cannot earn our way to heaven, it is Jesus Christ. If anyone knows we can't make it into the pool, it is Jesus. *We* are the man who has been infirm for thirty-eight years—sick and lost. Christ comes, and He says to you, "I want to do a miracle in your life. I want to change you. I am the only One who can do it. You have tried to change yourself. For thirty-eight years, you've been trying to get over there to the pool, but you can't do it.

"You don't have to try anymore," Jesus says to you and to me. "You just come, and let Me save you. I'll not only save you, but I'll sustain you. I'll see you right through to the kingdom. I'll give you newness of life, I'll resurrect you. You were physically and spiritually dead, but I'll resurrect you. And because I do resurrect you now spiritually, you will be a part of that great resurrection at the end time when I call all those who have believed in Me. And if you're then among those resting in the grave, you too will come forth."

Right now, Jesus offers all of this to you. As you reach the end of this chapter now, why not talk to the Healer near the pool, the Miracle Worker at Cana, the Lord of the Sabbath, the God who can do for you what you can never do for yourself?

Pray in your own words. Maybe something like this:

"Lord Jesus, please come into my life right now. Create a new heart within me. Bring this miracle to me. I have tried on my own, and I've failed. I now realize that I cannot save myself. You have to save me—and I thank You for doing it."

It took a miracle to create the universe—and that was fantastic— but when He saved my soul, cleansed and made me whole, it took a miracle of love and grace!

THE BREAD OF LIFE

This is what finally did it for them.

This is what sealed their certainty that He was the One.

Yes, they had seen Him heal people. They had heard Him as He taught. They had even seen Him raise the dead.

But after this one, they said to themselves, "This has to be the Messiah—the Chosen One, the King—the Deliverer who will free us from the oppression of Rome."

On this particular day, they had been listening to every word He said. But at some point, He tried to slip away from them. He'd gone around to the other side of the Sea of Galilee, but by the time He got there, they were already waiting for Him. They could not seem to get enough of Him.

Sometimes it's good to get away. Ministers, especially, I think, really begin to fail when they don't get away—when they don't take time to recharge and rejuvenate. They need to go somewhere and just do nothing, not because they want to be lazy, but because they've got to recharge their spiritual batteries. Reading about some of the great preachers of history, I find that they were invariably given at least six weeks and sometimes the entire summer off to read, study, and rebuild.

Peter Marshall—once chaplain of the U.S. Senate and whose

life was celebrated in the book and movie entitled *A Man Called Peter*—always spent the full summer out on Cape Cod outlining his entire sermon series—everything he was going to preach through the coming year. He saturated himself with Scripture and walked alone on the beach, reflecting, thinking, praying, and searching.

Men who are supposed to bring to others ideas, thoughts, and inspiration need that kind of time. Christ needed time away— He needed solitude. Even though He was the Messiah, He was also human. We see this great complexity in Jesus Christ, in which one moment, He's doing a great miracle, and the next moment, He is tired and needs time alone with His Father.

So here He was, preaching, teaching, and healing, while Philip, one of the disciples, was standing nearby. Jesus said, "These people are hungry—they need to be fed."

"Master," Philip replied, "we don't have any money. We only have a few dollars left in the treasury. There's no way on earth that we can feed all these people. And where out here would we get food, even if we had the money?"

They didn't have a McDonald's or a Wal-Mart right around the corner. They couldn't call Domino's Pizza and get thousands of pizzas delivered. We have to recognize the fact that if the people didn't bring it with them, they didn't have it.

The Bible says that what Jesus did, He did to test Philip. Philip was the spreadsheet and calculator type. An analytical personality, he would look at a situation like this and say, "We have so many dollars. There are yea so many people. So divide that into so many dollars and—we don't have it. So that's it."

Philip missed the idea of faith. He missed the idea of miracles. He missed what God can do when men will let Him. So the Bible says that Jesus said this to Philip to test him. Jesus is still testing *our* faith. What He wants us to do is often just a little bit beyond where we can reach.

When I was a young man, I remember a man by the name

of "Salty" Parker. He was the manager of the Dallas Eagles, a Double-A team in the Giants organization. Later, he went to the major leagues as a coach. Salty Parker was known for what he could do with a fungal bat. A fungal bat is a very thin bat used for hitting to the infield or hitting fly balls to the outfield. Not a bat you would ever use in a real game, it is used strictly for practice, and there is something about the fungal—maybe the thinness of it—that if you are really good, you can control the ball.

Salty Parker was known for being able to pretty much estimate a player's speed and to hit with that fungal just beyond their reach. But in trying to catch the ball, they had to run farther and faster than perhaps they had ever run before. The day that I had my own tryout for professional baseball, Salty Parker was hitting the fungal. Every ball was hit just beyond where I could reach. I never ran so hard in all my life! I ran so hard I tore the cleats off the bottom of my shoe, and I'd never done that before. I thought I had failed. But when I got back to the dressing room, he called me into his office, reached into his desk, and pulled out a contract. I hadn't failed.

Sometimes, this is the way it is with Jesus. He asks you to do something beyond your reach. You can't do it, but He can. Often, this may be a victory in your life He wants you to have!

Jesus was testing Philip. You remember the miracle? You remember what happened? A boy, some fish, and some bread—and the Master takes them and breaks that bread and those fish, and He continues breaking till He feeds five thousand men. He probably fed some fifteen thousand people in all, including the women and children.

Then the crowd tried to make him King. They said, "This is the One! This is the Messiah! This is the One who can lead us out from the oppression of Rome. We will make Him King, and He will restore Israel to the prominence we had under David and Solomon."

But, that's not exactly what Jesus had in mind. So they came and tried to take Him and force Him to be the Messiah they wanted—to release them from the oppression of Rome. The Bible says that He then disappeared.

His disciples got back into the boat and started across the lake, and a storm came up. Now, John doesn't go into much detail on the feeding of the five thousand or on the storm the disciples encountered, because the other Gospel writers do. John wrote this after the other Gospels were finished, and he knew there was no need to recount all the details, so he simply mentions them so we get the context of when this took place.

Because remember, John's message over and over again is that Jesus is God. Not that Jesus is a king, a prophet, or a teacher—though He was all of those. John's burden is that everyone see Jesus as the one and only true God! Jesus is the Savior. He's the Creator. He's the Light. He's the Living Water. He's everything—and there is nothing else. He is it. That's the message of John. Again, that's where John is headed in chapter 6.

So out on the lake, you remember that the storm came up. There they were, the disciples, and they were afraid. They were afraid because Jesus wasn't with them. They wanted to be with Him. You need to go back to Matthew to get a fuller picture, but you'll remember that Peter finally saw Jesus—walking on the stormy sea. Peter spontaneously jumped out of the water—he wanted to be with the Savior. Peter had a lot of problems, but he had some good traits—none better than that he always wanted to be with Jesus. Peter was the kind of fellow that if the Lord stopped abruptly, Peter was likely to run right into His back. He was always right there. He wanted to be with Jesus so much so that he did something without thinking—something else he often did. He jumped right into the water and began to walk to Jesus. And he succeeded too—until he took his eyes off Jesus. Then down he went!

Then they willingly received Him into the boat, and immediately the boat was at the land where they were going. On the following day, when the people who were standing on the other side of the sea saw that there was no other boat there, except that one which His disciples had entered, and that Jesus had not entered the boat with His disciples, but His disciples had gone away alone—however, other boats came from Tiberias, near the place where they ate bread after the Lord had given thanks—when the people therefore saw that Jesus was not there, nor His disciples, they also got into boats and came to Capernaum, seeking Jesus. And when they found Him on the other side of the sea, they said to Him, "Rabbi, when did You come here?"

Jesus answered them and said, "Most assuredly, I say to you, you seek Me, not because you saw the signs, but because you ate of the loaves and were filled. Do not labor for the food which perishes, but for the food which endures to everlasting life, which the Son of Man will give you, because God the Father has set His seal on Him."

Then they said to Him, "What shall we do, that we may work the works of God?" (verses 21–28).

Now, Jesus has just fed them the day before—a great miracle. He did it for them—they did not do it for themselves. Now they are coming back to Him and want to be fed again. He can look right into their minds. He knows exactly what they are thinking, and He says to them, "Listen, don't labor for food, which perishes." Even the food that He fed them had already perished. That food which He gave them was just food—even though it was miraculous food—but they were already hungry again.

"I'm telling you," He says to them, "don't worry about this food that you are going to take into your bodies. That's not the thing to think about, because that food is going to perish."

We do a lot of thinking about food that's going to perish. A couple of years ago, an article came out in one of the popular magazines, with a list of what they called superfoods. Number one on the list was broccoli, I remember. A friend of mine saw the list and jokingly said he kept looking for pizza, ice cream, and cake, and was very disappointed that they were not on the list!

Superfoods. We are interested in good, healthy food. I would not in any way detract from the importance of taking in good food. However, Christ is saying that far more important than what you take in through your mouth is what you take into your mind. More important than this physical food is the spiritual food you must know about.

A kind of food exists, Jesus told them, that endures forever, which is only available through the Son of man. Somehow, this passed right over their heads, and they came back with, " 'What shall we do, that we may work the works of God?' " (verse 28).

Man always wants to save himself. Jesus said clearly, "Don't labor for this bread." Their next question? "How do we do the works of God?" Incredible!

I've had people come to me after I've preached sermons with long lists, and they say, "I like it when you give us steps one, two, three, four, and five."

We all do! We would like a point-by-point checklist we can mark off, so we can then know we have life eternal. To the people in John's story—and to each of us today—Jesus said, " 'This is the work of God, that you believe in Him whom He sent' " (verse 29).

You want to know what your work is? Believe in Him. But, somebody says, the Bible states that even the devils believe—and tremble. That's right. But there's a difference in that belief and the belief Jesus talked about. It's the difference between just knowing that Jesus is a person—just knowing that He exists—and receiving Him as Savior, actually assimilating Him into your life. When that happens, a change takes place. A change that occurs, not by our trying somehow through human effort to make a change in ourselves, but through making the indwelling Christ so much a part of us that He is assimilated into our very beings—into our very personalities.

"Therefore they said to Him, 'What sign will You perform then, that we may see it and believe You? What work will You do? Our fathers ate the manna in the desert; as it is written, "He gave them bread from heaven to eat." ' Then Jesus said to them, 'Most assuredly, I say to you, Moses did not give you the bread from heaven, but My Father gives you the true bread from heaven' " (verses 30–32).

Beginning with His words in verse 27, Jesus led them step by step: Do not work. Moses gave you bread from heaven. And finally, He brought them to His desired destination in verse 35: " 'I am the bread of life.' "

Remember the woman at the well? Jesus told her that He was the Water of Life. Now, He's the Bread of Life. If you enter into this experience Jesus describes, He says you will never thirst. You'll never hunger. You see, they were only thinking about the next meal. But He's thinking about something so much deeper than that. He's talking about real soul thirst. Real soul hunger. We can actually sit on the great promises of Jesus and starve to death.

Some of you remember the story of a woman by the name of Hetty Green. When she died, her net worth was over one hundred million dollars. That's a few dollars more than most of us see in one place at one time! Just put that kind of money out at interest, and you could live far better than most of us live. But this woman lived like a pauper. She wore rags and wouldn't buy anything new.

Her son got a sore on his leg. She kept looking for a free clinic that would take her and her son, and not many free clinics want to take people who are worth one hundred million. Finally, by the time she got her son into one, she had wasted so much time that he lost his leg. She was rich. But she lived as if she were a pauper. Just having money doesn't make you wealthy—though using it for good purposes does.

A lot of people with a whole lot less money are far wealthier—far wealthier than was Hetty Green. To have money and not do anything good with it is such a waste. God doesn't built dams. He doesn't build reservoirs. In reference to money, L. H. Coleman has often said that if "God can get it through you, He'll get it to you." And I believe in that concept. But God doesn't like for us to dam things up and hold it back and not do anything good with it. He likes a real, living stream that's doing something good for people and for His kingdom. You go to the Sea of Galilee, and it's a truly beautiful sea. It is giving constantly, sending its water out as it takes in. But when that water goes down the Jordan River and hits the Dead Sea, the water stops. It gives no more. There's not one living thing in the Dead Sea. When we stop giving, we die.

Some of us are sitting on a fortune and do not realize it. Christ has offered us life eternal. He says to us, "I want to give you something so that you will never, never, ever need anything else again—and that is eternal life. I want to give you the Bread of Life. I want to free you from whatever is holding you down—from the struggles you are having. I want to free you from the clutches of sin. I have something for you." But we often just walk off and leave that which is so valuable that it's priceless.

In Titusville, Pennsylvania, a farmer with a little farm got a letter from his cousin that said, "Come up to Canada. Sell that lousy farm of yours down there, and come up here and help us. We are skimming coal oil off the lakes and rivers, and we are selling it and making lots of money."

So the farmer sold his farm. The county records show that he sold it for $833.00 and went to Canada. The man who bought the farm walked around his barn and found something strange. The farmer who had lived there had rigged up a paddlelike board to skim something black off the water so the cattle could drink the water. It was gathered in a low place, and the new farmer immediately recognized that this was oil. The great Pennsylvania oil find took place on the very farm that the farmer sold to seek his fortune somewhere else.

Some of us are looking for something, and we don't know what. And right here, all along, right in front of us, we have the fortune of all fortunes—life eternal. So often, we continue to struggle, and we do not find peace of mind. We don't find happiness. And I think Jesus is telling us why.

"Then Jesus said to them, 'Most assuredly, I say to you, unless you eat the flesh of the Son of Man and drink His blood, you have no life in you. Whoever eats My flesh and drinks My blood has eternal life, and I will raise him up at the last day.' . . . Therefore many of His disciples, when they heard this, said, 'This is a hard saying; who can understand it?' " (verses 53, 54, 60).

Drinking the blood of Jesus. Eating the flesh of Jesus. There's something about this that immediately turns us off. We don't like this kind of language, and when we read it, it seems strange. What can it possibly mean?

Well, first of all, it's not uncommon for us to use metaphors in our own society today. Winston Churchill during World War II talked about blood, sweat, and tears—right? Nobody accused him of anything strange when he said, "I have nothing to offer but blood, toil, tears, and sweat." And consider General Patton. What did they call him? "Old Blood and Guts," right?

In fact, if you study back into history, you will find that people sometimes used similar words when they had worked hard all day long. They would say, "I have eaten my flesh, and I have drunk my blood today."

Or, when a leader wanted your loyalty, he would say, "I want you to give me your flesh and blood—and I will take it."

Now Jesus is using the same language. Hard for them? Yes. Why? Because they simply did not want to do it. They knew that it meant commitment. It meant commitment beyond anything they had ever done before.

And we're no different than they were. We, too, are really afraid of commitment. We say, "Lord I want to be saved—I really do want to be saved. So save me, but just don't mess with my life. I've got things all planned. I want to do it my way."

One reason we do not have the happiness and fulfillment we want in life is that we have not allowed our thoughts to be His thoughts, our will to be His will, and our plans to be His plans. We have not allowed Him to come into our lives—to permeate our lives in such a way as to change us from the inside out.

We like to make our changes from the outside in. We can just change a few things, tack on a few nice phrases, and get rid of a few old habits—and then we can call ourselves Christians. But Jesus says, "No. I don't want you to do that. You must take My life inside you. Your thinking, your brain, your emotions, your physical body—all must be in tune with Me."

Full commitment means taking Jesus in and allowing His Holy Spirit to come in and control us. My friend, when we do this, suddenly we will begin to see a real difference in the Christian life. It doesn't mean that there will be no more problems. Hardly. We'll always have problems. But the difference is that without Jesus, we are struggling with the problems. We are trying to solve the problems ourselves, and we go on with that struggle. Every single one of us has that tendency.

You have many problems with which you've struggled. And when they hit you right between the eyes, your first impulse is to begin to struggle. But then you say, "Wait a minute. These aren't mine. Not anymore. They used to be my struggles, but now they are not. They are God's. He has come in, and I'm going to turn them over to Him."

And suddenly, all those old struggles that used to pull us down and upset us and disturb us and stop us and discourage us, suddenly they just don't have the same power they used to have. The amazing thing is that all of us want to try to solve our problems ourselves, but have you ever noticed how few you can actually solve yourself?

What Jesus describes is not imitating Him—it's assimilating Him. We take in His Spirit, His life, absorbing Him into our very being. His teachings, His character, His ways, His virtues, and His wisdom all becomes ours.

You see somebody with a big white suit and a cape, long sideburns, and black hair, and you know who he's imitating, don't you? There are a lot of Elvis imitators around. But the idea is not to imitate Jesus Christ, not to try to act like Jesus Christ, but to actually assimilate Jesus Christ through the Word. You remain you, with your own personality. Yet in a different and unique way, every one of us portrays Jesus Christ. Christ within, coming out to be seen on the outside.

If you have heard me tell this story before or have read it in one of my books, indulge me as I share it again. It's had a big impact on me, so I've told it many times. One day, when I was a student in college, I went into Cleburne, Texas, to get a haircut at a barbershop that was a favorite with some of the students.

I liked this certain barber, and as he was cutting my hair and we were talking, I looked out the plate glass window and saw a lady walking by. This lady was dressed in rags. She had a sack slung over her back, and she pulled it down to get some things out of a little trash can that was there—obviously a "bag lady," as we call them. Then she reached over and picked up a still-lighted cigarette butt somebody had thrown out, and she began to smoke the rest of that thing. She coughed and sounded so sick. My heart went out to her, and I asked the barber, "Why doesn't somebody help her?"

"Well," he replied, "that's quite a story. She lives in a little shack down across the railroad tracks. She had one son and nobody knew who the father was. When it came time for her boy to go to school, she didn't want to send him. But the officials prevailed, and they took him to school. When he got there, he was afraid—shy—as he had never been allowed around people much. He had poor clothes and no shoes. So the teachers got him some shoes and some clean clothes, and they cleaned him up.

"Somewhere about halfway through the first grade," the barber continued, "they began to realize that this was a very bright child. Second grade, he really got into it. Third grade, he was getting there at the same time the janitor did in the morning, and he would help open the school. He would help the janitor, and he was the delight of the whole school—everybody loved him. By the time this boy hit high school, he was the most popular kid in school, and he really was an excellent student, all around.

"He went looking for a job in high school and went all around the town. He knew now that he had to try to make some money. He wanted to live differently from the way he had been living, so he found a job at the bank. They said, 'Can you come in and do the cleaning?' So he did that every afternoon after school.

"When he graduated from high school, they said to him, 'What are you going to do now?' He said, 'I would like to go to a university and get a degree.' The owner of the bank said, 'Here's what we'll do. We'll pay your way, if you'll come back here to work for us when you're through.' So they struck a deal. The young man went off to school and got a degree and came back and started working full time at the bank—first as a teller, then as a loan officer, and now, he is the executive vice president of the largest bank here in town. And do you know," the barber added, "when she is digging through that garbage can out there, she is no more than seven or eight feet from her son's office in the bank through the brick wall next to the trash can."

"Why doesn't he do something for his mother?" I asked the barber.

"Ah," he said, "he's tried. When he first started making money, he'd take something down to her to wear. He'd say, 'Mom, here's a dress. I bought it for you, please wear this.' And she would say,

'Oh, so what I have is not good enough for you?' And she'd throw the new dress outside and have nothing to do with it. He'd take her food and leave it there and say, 'Mom, please eat this. I'll feed you, Mama—I'll get whatever you need.' But again, she'd have nothing to do with anything he brought.

"When he started working full time at the bank, he found a little house—a nice and neat little house with a little white picket fence around it—and he went to his mother and said, 'Mom, I found a place I want to show to you. Please let me show you this place. I want you to move into this house.' She said, 'You get out of here and don't come back. This is my home—this is where I live—and if it is not good enough for you, then it's just too bad, because this is where I'm staying.' "

"So you mean he can't do anything for her?" I responded in amazement.

"He's tried over and over," the barber explained, "and everybody knows that he can't do anything for her."

That day as I left the barbershop, I walked across that street. As I stopped right in the middle of the street to wait for some cars to pass, I'll never forget the impression that suddenly came over me. I thought how that old woman is just like we all are in this world. Christ comes to us, and He says, "I want to give you the Bread of Life. I want to give you this Bread that will result in life eternal. I want you to have it."

"Oh, no thanks, Lord," too many of us say. "I want to keep searching through the garbage cans Satan has to offer—and I'll do it on my own."

Jesus comes along and says to us, "I want to give you a mansion—a mansion that would make the mansions of this earth look like shacks in comparison."

"Oh, no thanks," we tell Him. "No pie in the sky for me. None of that—I'll take what I can get here."

Jesus comes along and says, "Won't you take My robe of righteousness? I want to give it to you—my robe of perfect righteousness—as a gift to you. You can have it."

"You know," too often He hears, "I think I'm pretty good, thanks. I think this old coat I've got on is all right."

We go along in our filthy rags, turning down Christ's robe of righteousness. He wants to save us. He wants to change us. He doesn't want us to be imitators of Him—He wants us to actually assimilate Him into our very being.

Our words should be the very words of Peter here in this chapter. All the other people had gone away, and Jesus said to His twelve disciples, " 'Do you also want to go away?' But Simon Peter answered Him, 'Lord, to whom shall we go? You have the words of eternal life' " (verses 67, 68).

There is no other place to go.

Jesus is the one Friend who will see you through.

Jesus is not only the Companion for our journey—He is our Destination.

THE LIGHT OF THE WORLD

OK, we've now gone seven full chapters into this book, and I need to see if you've been paying attention.

What is the central message John is trying to get across in his Gospel?

If you said that John's message is that Jesus is God, you get a gold star next to your name. As one of my old professors used to say, "If you can get that into your head, you've got it in a nutshell." And he was right, you know! You get that into your mind, and you have the real essence of the book of John.

In this chapter, I'd like to focus on John, chapter 8. But rather than beginning at verse 1, we'll start at verse 12, move on toward the end, and then if the printer will give us enough pages, we can come back and pick up the earlier verses.

"Then Jesus spoke to them again, saying, 'I am the light of the world. He who follows Me shall not walk in darkness, but have the light of life' " (John 8:12).

Come with me to the Feast of Tabernacles. A lot of ceremonies happened during this great annual celebration. One took place each morning when the priest went from the temple to the pool of Salome, filled a golden pitcher, and took it back to the temple altar, as the people sang praises from the psalms—particularly Psalm 114, the psalm that says,

Tremble, O earth, at the presence of the Lord,
At the presence of the God of Jacob,
Who turned the rock into a pool of water,
The flint into a fountain of waters (verses 7, 8).

The people celebrated the time when God led Moses through the wilderness to the rock from which water flowed. In doing so, the Israelites celebrated the Water of Life.

Earlier in John's Gospel, Jesus said to the Samaritan woman: " 'Whoever drinks of this water will thirst again, but whoever drinks of the water that I shall give him will never thirst. But the water that I shall give him will become in him a fountain of water springing up into everlasting life' " (John 4:13, 14).

Then in John 6, Jesus is the Manna from heaven—the Bread of Life. And now here in John 8, Jesus is the Light of the world.

Water. Bread. Light.

While the morning ceremony of the Feast of Tabernacles focused on the water, the evening ceremony was all about the light. In the courtyard, they set alight two giant torches, so bright they could be seen all across Jerusalem. This was to symbolize the pillar of fire by night that accompanied the children of Israel in the wilderness for forty years.

Jesus, at the Feast, joined the others looking at this dazzling light, and I believe that it was in that very setting that He said, " 'I am the light of the world' " (John 8:12). The people could not really comprehend this. What does He mean—He is the Light of the world?

That's *exactly* what Jesus is! Jesus has always existed—and that's the message of John. "In Him was life, and the life was the light of men. And the light shines in the darkness, and the darkness did not comprehend it. . . . That was the true Light which gives light to every man coming into the world" (John 1:4, 5, 9).

When this world was spoken into existence back at the very beginning, Jesus was the One whose voice spoke the world into existence. The message of John is that when Christ came into this world, He was not a new being. He was God—unequivocally and completely; He had always existed. Jesus is part of the Trinity—Father, Son, and Holy Spirit—who have existed from all eternity.

Jesus is God. Jesus is the Creator. And Jesus is the Light of the world.

To the Israelites, the light symbolized the very presence of God Himself. During their wilderness wanderings, the pillar of fire was their protection. At the time they left Egypt, it stood between them and the Egyptians that first night and kept them from being destroyed. The Light—the presence of God.

Through Jesus Christ, we have the assurance of the presence of God with us. When Christians pray together, God Himself is there with us. The presence of God, symbolized by that pillar of fire by night and that cloud by day, is still with us today. Jesus still says, "I am the Light of the world." You may not see that light. You may not see a pillar of fire, as did Israel. But Jesus is present.

As Israel spent years in the Sinai desert, the summer heat was stifling—130, maybe 140 degrees or more. Yet God protected His children from that heat. And the desert is a place of extremes. It can be just as cold at night as it becomes hot during the day. Jesus was Israel's protection—from the heat, from the cold, from the wild animals, and from their enemies.

While the pillar of fire by night and cloud by day meant protection to Israel, it also meant guidance. When the cloud moved, the children of Israel were to move with it. It would hover over the tabernacle, and as it stayed there, they stayed and camped—sometimes for a few days, sometimes for thirty days, sometimes for longer. And then, when the pillar moved, they followed.

We need to understand today that God is still leading in our lives. We need to listen and watch—to look for His direction and be willing to follow rather than run ahead of Him, as we're so prone to do. In fact, God gave Israel exact directions. He said they were to stay about three-fifths of a mile back from the cloud, so they did not miss the direction in which the cloud was leading. Sometimes we get so close, so quickly, that we're actually not following the cloud. We miss the direction the Lord wants us to move. We need to stay back and watch and wait a while for the direction of God, till we can clearly see that direction.

That is a lesson many of us have never really learned—how to ascertain whether or not we're actually following God, rather than running ahead of Him. We need to know, first of all, which direction we are already heading in our life. I think the main way you can find that is simply on your knees—but also by watching for the leading of God's providence.

"You should teach," a pastor told a man in his congregation.

"But I can't teach," the man protested.

"No, you really should teach."

"But you didn't hear me, pastor," the man replied. "I told you I can't teach."

"Have you ever tried to teach?"

"No, I haven't."

"Then you don't know," the pastor insisted, "whether you can teach or not!"

"Well, I just don't feel I can teach."

"I have a class I want you to teach," the pastor answered. "I am convinced you can teach—that you have what it takes, and I want you to start teaching this class."

So the man began to teach, and he quickly began to grow as a teacher. He soon discovered that he actually did have the gift of teaching.

Sometimes other people can see in you what you cannot see in yourself. Listen to their direction. Listen to their counsel. Sometimes they just may be directing you in the right way. Now, don't listen to just everybody. Make sure you are listening to the right kind of person, and don't necessarily listen to one isolated individual. But if several people tell you, "I think you should teach," or "I think you should go into the ministry," or "Have you thought about medicine?"—then maybe you need to listen to that. Perhaps the Lord is leading you through godly people and what they say.

Watch for the direction of the cloud, so that you may follow. You see, Christ is not only interested in leading the whole group, He's interested in leading you personally. So ask yourself, "Does this possibility in any way conflict with my belief in God and in His Word?"

You know, sometimes that's ruled out a lot of things for me right away. I've wanted to do certain things in my life, then looked at them, and no—I could not do those things and be in harmony with God's Word. So that has to go. That's no longer an option. I might want to do it, but it is not an option for me. So you weed those things out, and then, as you look into the Word of God, it is amazing how God speaks to you through His Word. He speaks to you through people—and He speaks to you through His Word. Just simply as you're studying and reading the Word, you will see and receive direction.

I know that when I talk about that, some people think about it and say, "Well, I've never had that happen to me." That kind of leading and guidance doesn't happen all the time. It doesn't happen every moment. But it will happen if you continue to read the Word of God while saying, "Lord, lead me. I don't know where to go. I don't know exactly what You want me to do. I don't know what is best for my life. So lead me and direct me." And He'll do it through His Word. He will do it.

So guidance is one way in which Jesus is the Light of the world. You see, we're out in darkness, and we're looking at our lives and wondering, "Father, what do You want me to do?" I'll tell you what He wants you to do. He wants you to make the most of that marriage you're in right now—not leave it and try again with someone else. He wants you to make the most of the situation you are in right now. The grass is always greener on the other side of the fence, until you get to the other side of the fence. If you jump the fence, to get to the greener grass, you'll find that the grass on the other side has to be mowed just as did the grass you left behind!

Take that situation you are in today and make it work. That's what God wants you to do. He wants you to take the job you are in right now and turn it into something exciting for Him and for you and your life. You see, He's given every single one of us some kind of job to do in this world, and it should not be just a mundane thing. If it is, then you may need either to rejuvenate your job or to find at least some good hobby or sideline you can be excited about.

I have a good friend who has a job that is very mundane, but on the side, do you know what he does? He preaches. He's a layman, and he started out teaching a class, then preaching, and now they have him pastoring a church. He goes to his mundane job eight hours a day and does a good job. But the excitement of his life is not those eight hours a day—even though he's found there a lot of people to whom he's able to minister. The real excitement of his life is the rest of the week, when he's ministering to individuals.

Christ, the Light of the world. When you're out there in the darkness, Christ will light it up, and He'll lead you out of that darkness, if you'll let Him do it. That's a major part of the message in the eighth chapter of John. It's a beautiful, beautiful message. In fact, Jesus as the Light of the world is one of the great "I AM" statements. There are twenty-three in all, such as:

" 'I am the bread of life' " (John 6:35).
" 'I am the light of the world' " (8:12).
" 'I am the door' " (10:9).
" 'I am the way, the truth, and the life' " (14:6).

The great I AM. And to the Jews, these words of Jesus seemed to be blasphemy. He's saying, " 'Before Abraham was' " (8:58),

" 'I am the good shepherd' " (10:11).
" 'I am the resurrection and the life' " (11:25).
" 'I am the true vine' " (15:1).

The very center, again, is Jesus. He says, "I AM." And He is!

You know something? When we read these texts, we can do one of two things with them. We can take the Bible and begin to believe that Jesus Christ is really who He says He is—or we can reject Him. One or the other—there is no in-between choice. And there may be battles as we make our choice.

What if you—or I—walked into a room, and said, "I am the light of the world." That would be the most ridiculous statement anybody could make, wouldn't it? And it would be for Jesus too—unless He is. Not just a good teacher would make that statement. Not just a good philosopher would make that statement. Not just a good man. He's either demented—or He's God. One or the other—no in between.

So as you look at the book of John, you may wrestle with these things. When Jesus spoke some of these things, John says that "when they heard this, [they] said, 'This is a hard saying;' . . . many of His disciples went back and walked with Him no more" (verses 60, 66). We either go with Him, or we don't. If we go with Him, then we enter into the belief He spoke of.

"Then Jesus said to those Jews who believed Him, 'If you abide in My word, you are My disciples indeed. And you shall know the truth, and the truth shall make you free.' They answered Him, 'We are Abraham's descendants, and have never been in bondage to anyone. How can You say, "You will be made free"?' Jesus answered them, 'Most assuredly, I say to you, whoever commits sin is a slave of sin' " (verses 31–34).

That makes all of us slaves, doesn't it? Outside of Christ, all of us are slaves.

"And a slave does not abide in the house forever, but a son abides forever. Therefore if the Son makes you free, you shall be free indeed.

"I know that you are Abraham's descendants, but you seek to kill Me, because My word has no place in you. I speak what I have seen with My Father, and you do what you have seen with your father."

They answered and said to Him, "Abraham is our father." Jesus said to them, "If you were Abraham's children, you would do the works of Abraham.

"But now you seek to kill Me, a Man who has told you the truth which I heard from God. Abraham did not do this.

"You do the deeds of your father." Then they said to Him, "We were not born of fornication; we have one Father—God."

Jesus said to them, "If God were your Father, you would love Me, for I proceeded forth and came from God; nor have I come of Myself, but He sent Me.

"Why do you not understand My speech? Because you are not able to listen to My word.

"You are of your father the devil, and the desires of your father you want to do. He was a murderer from the beginning, and does not stand in the truth, because there is no truth in him. When he speaks a lie, he speaks from his own resources, for he is a liar and the father of it.

"But because I tell the truth, you do not believe Me.

"Which of you convicts Me of sin? And if I tell the truth, why do you not believe Me?

"He who is of God hears God's words; therefore you do not hear, because you are not of God" (verses 35–47).

"Why don't you believe Me?" Jesus asked. That's the question to us today. Why don't we believe Him? Oh, we say, we DO believe Him.

In 1824, a man was born in France by the name of Jean François Gravelet. Later, he changed his name to the stage name Charles Blondin or "The Great Blondin"—and became famous for walking tightropes. You've likely heard this story already many times.

Blondin used to stretch ropes across Niagara Falls and walk across them. One time he took a wheelbarrow across with a person in it. Another time, he went out to the middle and stopped. Have you ever been to Niagara Falls? It's not the kind of place where you want to walk out to the halfway point on a cable and just stand out there.

In fact, my wife and I went there soon after we were married, though not on our honeymoon. We only had a one-day honeymoon. We couldn't afford the second day, so we came home. But we went there sometime during the first year or so of our marriage, and I couldn't even get my wife to look over the side at the falls. I'm wanting to look at Niagara Falls, but she didn't care about it at all. We didn't stay there long, I guarantee you!

But here was this man Blondin out there, cooking an omelet at the middle of a cable. He cooked it there and ate it. Another time, he took a man on his shoulders and walked across. When he got to the other side, Blondin looked at one man in the crowd and asked, "Do you believe that I could carry you across?"

"Yes," the man replied. "I just saw you carry him."

"Then get on my shoulders," said Blondin.

"Oh, no—no," the man answered.

The fact is that sometimes we say we believe in Jesus—but we're afraid to get on His shoulders. We are afraid to let Him lead us where He would lead us in our lives. We're afraid to trust Him with everything in our life. This was the same problem Jesus found with the Jews. "You don't believe Me." Now, some of these people had really been following Him. They had been listening to His teaching and eating the bread and seeing the miracles. But when it came down to really saying, "This is our God, and we're going to follow Him," they couldn't do it.

Jesus said, "You don't believe Me." And if you are not willing to get on the rope—if you are not willing to walk out with Him—it may just be that you don't believe. Jesus says, "You are slaves to sin. But the truth will make you free. And if you will, I will make you free."

Don't you want victory over sin? Don't you want it? You see, if Christ has come into our hearts, He gives us that desire to have victory. Now, that may not mean that we have that victory. We are human. You see, this whole thing would work perfectly if it weren't for the fact that we are human. Linking up with Christ, theoretically, we could all have total victory. The problem is, I'm not a theory, and neither are you. I'm blood and flesh. I respond as any human being would, and sometimes that's not the right way to respond.

Christ says, "I want to come into your life and take control," and in direct proportion to how fully we give Him control, we will see victory take place in our lives. As we read through this chapter in John, we see that this is exactly what He promised—exactly what He did.

Now, before we leave this chapter, come back with me to the first few verses. Here, we find a set up situation. Some of the religious leaders have contrived to set up a trap for Jesus. They are trying to trip Him up. They are trying to get Him to say, "Stone her"—the "her" being a woman they also set up to be caught in adultery.

"Moses said to stone her," they maintained, "so don't You agree we should go ahead and stone her?" How could Jesus say No and go against the Law of Moses?

I can just see this woman in my imagination—clothes torn from being dragged through the streets; shame and fear in her eyes. And immediately we see the character of Jesus Christ. We see His understanding. We see His compassion. We see His forgiveness.

Christ looks down at her, stoops over, and begins to write in the dust at His feet. He begins to list the sins of some of the men standing there with sharp stones in their hands. You see, everybody there that day was a sinner. Not just the woman accused of adultery—but the scribes and Pharisees too were sinners. Some of those very men may have been responsible for the woman's sin—may have led her into it.

As you visualize this scene, somewhere there, you can place yourself in the picture. You see, we are all in that picture somewhere. Christ stooped and began to write in that sand, and I don't know exactly what He wrote, but it included the sins of the others standing there. For a moment, He stood up and said, " 'He who is without sin among you, let him throw a stone at her first' " (verse 7). Then He stooped down and continued His writing.

Then came the sound of stones dropping and footsteps, as the accusers turned and walked away in embarrassment. What they should have done was to stay. They each should have said, "Lord, please forgive me for my sin."

Jesus is telling us here how to treat those who have unfortunate circumstances—those who have fallen into sin. Sometimes we get the idea that we are to treat sinners harshly—that if we don't, we are somehow condoning sin. Christ said "No, that's not true at all." So if anybody ever gets on your case for being compassionate to someone who has sinned—who has fallen— there may be a lot of things you can tell them. But one thing that for sure you can tell them is that in John, chapter 8, Christ taught us how to treat those who have fallen.

A while back, I was in a church out west, sitting in a pastor's study, and he was telling me about some of the things he was facing.

"There is a teenage girl who's pregnant," he said. "And that's an automatic."

"What?" I asked, not understanding him.

"That's an automatic," he repeated.

"An automatic *what?*" I asked.

"Oh, it's an automatic disfellowshiping," he said.

"Are you kidding me?" I replied. "That should be an automatic act of love and forgiveness, not an automatic disfellowshiping."

I don't believe in automatic disfellowships. It's ridiculous. You see, when someone falls, that's the time when we as church members should demonstrate that we are a loving, caring church; to say, "We do have the spirit of the Lord Jesus Christ in our lives. We can stand with you. We will stand with you. We will not condemn you. We don't condone sin—no! Because Christ did not condone sin. He hated sin, and we hate sin, but *we don't hate sinners*. Not any of them—and particularly not those who are members of our congregation." So with Jesus, we should say that we love and care.

" 'Woman, where are those accusers of yours? Has no one condemned you?' She said, 'No one, Lord.' And Jesus said to her, 'Neither do I condemn you; go and sin no more' " (verses 10, 11). The New International Version says, " 'Go now and leave your life of sin.' " Jesus didn't tell her to go—and keep sinning.

The clear message of this story is that God loves you—and He loves me. Somewhere in that scene, each of us can be found. We are either on the ground as the sinner, or we're standing there as the accuser, or we're in the watching crowd. Wherever we are, we need the same mercy, the same forgiveness, that Jesus showed that day. We're not worthy of it—not one of us. He alone is worthy. But the amazing thing about the love of God that flowed through Jesus—that still does—is that His love is not for the worthy but for the unworthy. His forgiveness is only for the undeserving.

That is good news. Because it means we qualify!

Chapter 9 — John 9

THE BLIND MAN CALLS THEIR BLUFF

I really like the blind man (visually challenged, if we're being politically correct) that John tells us about in chapter 9. This is one clearly independent man. He has stumbled around Jerusalem all his life, unable to see. To have that kind of disability either makes a person very dependent—or very independent.

I love to travel in Israel and have done so many times. I know the area so well that I can travel—and have—from Dan to Beer-sheba without a map. *Oh, you're bragging,* you might think—but in Texas they say, "It ain't bragging if it's true!" When you know the area and have been there many times—when you get to certain places—you will see certain faces, and it seems they are always there, as if it's their territory.

This is especially true of the peddlers and beggars. If you don't see them, you start wondering where they are. They also have amazing memories. If you have made a number of trips there, they will remember and recognize you, especially if you are a generous tipper!

On one trip I had a group of young, energetic ministers along. We had flown all day and arrived late in the evening, and frankly, I was ready for bed. But these young ministers wanted to go out exploring that night. They had never been there before, and I was not about to let them go alone.

Pastor M. D. Lewis, a great Bible teacher and student of God's Word, was along, and he joined us for that midnight walk up to the Mount of Olives. We walked along the crest and then down the route that was most likely taken by Jesus when He made His triumphant entry on Palm Sunday—passing the Garden of Gethsemane, then up the hill to the Old City of Jerusalem, and along the Via Dolorosa.

As we left the Old City, a beggar was sitting by the gate. I had seen him many times before but always during the day. Now, here he was late at night at the same place. It seemed as if that beggar was *always* there.

The man born blind was that kind of person. Everybody in town knew him. They had all seen him, sitting at his spot. He was like part of the scenery, taken for granted and hardly noticed by those who passed each day.

Being blind must be a monumental challenge. Before they had children, my daughter Maryann and her husband, Kirk Krueger, were volunteers for the Christian Record Braille Foundation ski camps. Every winter, they would help at a ski camp in Colorado, and Kirk and Maryann would take their vacation and go there to work with those blind youth.

These young people might not have been able to see, but they still wanted to ski. Most were totally blind—all were legally blind. The counselors would use different techniques to help them ski. Usually, they would stand tight behind their student with their skis almost locked together, as they would go downhill. Some were skilled enough that all they needed was someone to ski next to them and guide them by voice, giving commands, such as "A little to your left," or "Make a hard right." Down the hill together they would go. Skiing is not without its dangers. But some have said that fewer of these skiers are injured than skiers who are sighted.

One year, our daughter Amy joined Kirk and Maryann for a few days at the blind ski camp. She was approached and asked to help with a snowmobile up the mountain. Amy agreed, the blind person climbed on behind her, and up the mountain they went.

When they arrived at the top, the leader said, "Now it is time for the blind person to drive." Amy later told me, "But Dad, that was difficult." She didn't know if she really wanted to do this or not. Finally, she agreed and got on the snowmobile behind the blind person, giving directions on which way to turn. She said it was quite an experience, trusting someone who cannot see anything to steer a snowmobile and have it go in the right direction, making sure not to confuse right from left!

Losing your sight does not mean that you cannot live a very active and productive life. One recent inspiration to me is a young lady who often sings on 3ABN and gives concerts across the country—Stephanie Dawn. Stephanie is not only blind, she has other health struggles too. But she is determined to share her faith through song. To me that makes her beautiful singing voice even more beautiful. God bless you, Stephanie Dawn!

In years past I have known many who did not let being blind stop them. The most difficult may have been those who lost their sight later in life. One of these was my former conference president, Pastor G. H. Rustad. This did not keep him from giving Bible studies—many by recording the studies on cassette and mailing them to people he had met on his trips. He had a very productive ministry in his retirement years, even while coping with blindness.

Many times our pastors look for an Adventist ghetto, where they feel comfortable with a community of other former workers. LeRoy Leiske, well-known church leader and former president of Pacific Press® Publishing Association—the publisher of this book—used to jokingly say, "When I retire, I'm going to move to Keene, Texas, and go down to the post office [where people would see each other when they got their mail and stop to talk] and see how much trouble I can cause the brethren [meaning the conference and church leaders]."

Now, of course, he was kidding! But too many former pastors live unproductive lives in retirement. Even though he was blind, Pastor Rustad wasn't one of those.

Someone came to Helen Keller one time and said, "Isn't it terrible to be blind?" Helen answered, "It is better to be blind and see with your heart than to have two good eyes and see absolutely nothing." Jesus spoke of the religious leaders of His day as the blind guides of the blind (see Matthew 15:14).

In John, chapter 8, we find Jesus teaching in the temple and saying some very strong things about Himself. He said, " 'I am the light of the world' " (verse 12), and then, to cap it off, in 8:58–9:2, we find this exchange, "Jesus said to them, 'Most assuredly, I say to you, before Abraham was, I AM.' Then they took up stones to throw at Him; but Jesus hid Himself and went out of the temple, going through the midst of them, and so passed by. Now as Jesus passed by, He saw a man who was blind from birth. And His disciples asked Him, saying, 'Rabbi, who sinned, this man or his parents, that he was born blind?' "

A rabbinical teaching held that if one had a disability, either the afflicted person or his parents had sinned to cause it. The Bible said that this man, though, was blind from birth. So you would think that this would rule out his sin as a cause. Certainly there was no way he could have sinned before he was born. But according to rabbinical teaching, he could! The Pharisees believed the teaching that some of the rabbis had developed—that there could be prenatal sin—and they taught this.

You've heard of prenatal care—well, now you've heard of prenatal sin. Many of the rabbis taught that it was possible for an infant to sin even in the mother's womb. Many of their teachings had been influenced by the Greek philosophy of Plato and others—ideas with no scriptural basis at all. These teachings had simply been worked out by the rabbis themselves and were taught as truth, even though they were not biblically supported.

So when the disciples posed this question, " 'Who sinned, this man or his parents?' " (9:1), they were asking a question to which many people both then and later would want to know the answer to. I am so glad they asked it, because Jesus takes care of this question forever, " 'Neither this man nor his parents sinned' " (verse 3).

Often people wonder, *What's wrong? Why is this illness or this problem happening to me? What did I do to deserve all of this trouble?* We need to understand from how Jesus related to the man born blind that just because problems occur in life, this does not necessarily mean that they come to us as a result of our own personal sinful choices.

Now, a lot of discussion has taken place about the translation of this text in John 9—verse 3. "Jesus answered, 'Neither this man nor his parents sinned, but that the works of God should be revealed in him.' "A misunderstanding of this text can cause even more distress than to think that sin brings on our problems—for this passage seems to say that this man's blindness happened so that Jesus would be glorified by performing this miracle.

You remember that the English punctuation of the Bible—as well as the chapter and verse divisions—came at the time of the King James translation (still my favorite for the beauty of the Old English). So there are a number of ways that this verse can be punctuated. For instance, in the NIV translation, we still have the same problem that we have in the King James and the New King James. " 'But this happened so that the work of God might be displayed in his life. As long as it is day, we must do the work of him who sent me. Night is coming, when no one can work. While I am in the world, I am the light of the world' " (verses 3–5, NIV).

Several noted instances are found in the Bible where scholars rightfully question the placing of a period or a comma, which can change the meaning of a text. One notable instance is where Jesus said to the thief on the cross, " 'I say to you, today you will be with Me in Paradise' " (Luke 23:43). By placing the comma *before* the word *today* instead of *after,* the text seems to say that the thief went to Paradise that very day. With the comma after the word *today,* the entire meaning changes. *Today* now refers to the day Jesus said this to the thief—not to when the thief would go to Paradise.

Punctuation can help us here in John 9:3 as well. " 'Neither this man nor his parents sinned. [Place a period right there after the word *sinned,* instead of a comma, and begin a new sentence.] But that the works of God should be revealed in him, [Place a comma right there after a word *him,* instead of a period.] I must work the works of Him who sent Me while it is day' " (verses 3, 4). By changing the punctuation, you have made this text to be completely in harmony with the rest of Scripture. This is not changing the words of the Bible—only the punctuation. And the punctuation, remember, was added centuries after the Bible was written.

So Jesus is saying, "I can work the works right now, even though they are chasing Me and want to kill Me. And someday they will, so we don't have much time and have to work while we still have the time. We can't wait, we can't put it off, time is short!"

It is out of harmony with our understanding of God that He would make this one man blind, just so that He could heal him. There were plenty of blind people around. God didn't have to make this one blind, so that Jesus would be in the right place at the right time to make this point—or so that God could get the glory.

Now, the Calvinists don't like this way of understanding this passage. They prefer the punctuation in the KJV and NIV much better, believing that God would indeed do that kind of thing. They also believe that God will torture sinners without ceasing for billions and trillions of years!

We see all around us sorrow, sadness, agony, and problems, and as Christians, these just as often touch us too. No one should ever tell a Christian that they will not have affliction, sorrow, trouble, agony, and pain—because every Christian will. Coming to Jesus doesn't mean that all of our problems will cease—not at all. It does mean that we will not have to face them alone, but that the Lord will walk through those valleys with us. Trials and tribulations can be great opportunities for displaying God's grace in us. Problems often destroy unbelievers, but problems should strengthen believers. It should cause believers to shine even brighter.

My good friend, Pastor Henry Barron, enjoys polishing rocks. Starting out with rough, misshapen, ugly rocks, he puts them in a tumbler that has special sand inside. As the tumbler begins to rotate, it polishes the rocks, until they become beautiful, smooth, and very attractive stones.

We may not enjoy the tumbling that life brings. Nevertheless, if we allow Him, God can use the polishing process, though not enjoyable, to help us develop character. So stay in the tumbler, be patient with the process, and in the end, you will be pleased with the result. So will be those around you who see in you the reflection of our Lord and Savior, Jesus Christ.

I have seen far too many people at death's door—believers and nonbelievers alike. I've seen both saints and sinners die. And it is so much easier to watch a saint die. Of course, a saint is just a sinner who has asked the Lord to come into his life and accepted Christ's merits in place of his own total lack of merits. A sinner tries to stand in his own merit, and of course, that's never enough!

Roger Holley was a saint. But even saints get sick. Roger had cancer, and I have never personally seen anyone in worse condition and still be alive, as was the case with Roger the last few weeks of his life. Yet his faith and commitment to the Lord was strong. The same was true of his friend and mentor Fordyce Detamore—who was likewise stricken with cancer. When I talked with Fordyce on the phone, he assured me that his trust in the Lord was as strong as ever and that he looked forward to the resurrection.

These men and a host of others have walked through the valley of the shadow of death without the fear that those without the Lord often possess. The agony I have witnessed at the deathbed of many unbelievers is not a pretty sight. There is no comparison between the believer and the unbeliever, when it comes to those moments.

Sometimes life hits us with a terrible blow. At those times, the world should see how a Christian can live not only in good times but in times of adversity as well. And how, in life with its ups and downs, a Christian's faith is still as strong—as he faces death—as it is in life. The living part is a challenge as well, because it is often easier to die than it is to live! Jesus showed us how to live. Even though He was getting away from those who would stone Him, He took time to stop and address the problems of the man born blind.

I believe that Jesus wants us, as He and the good Samaritan did, to be willing to help people in need, even though at times it may be a risk to our own safety. We have a Christian responsibility to help whenever we can. Now, you and I can't solve every problem of every single person, but we can help solve one, at least now and then. If each of us would reach out and help somebody, we would begin to see not only a difference in those we help but a difference in us.

I heard about a minister who finished up a meeting at his church late one night. He had sent his wife home with the car, thinking that he would get a ride with one of the members who were staying by to counsel with him after the service. But one by one, they left, and by the time he was ready to start for home, it was 2:00 A.M.—and he was alone at the church. Not wishing to disturb his wife, he decided to walk, though to do so meant walking through a very rough neighborhood.

Part of the way home, he happened to look into an alley, and huddled there, he saw a pathetic individual. He didn't know what the situation was, but he knew it was bad, and in his heart, he cried out to God: *Oh, God, why is the world the way that it is? Why do we have these kinds of situations? God, do You really see and know what is happening on this earth?*

And in his heart, the answer came back, *"Yes, I see!"*

Then why don't You do something about it?

And the minister said the answer came back, *"I just did. I brought it to your attention."*

God wants us to be involved in helping Him alleviate suffering in this world. We are His hands, His feet, and His heart of love. According to our abilities, we can do what we can to reach out and lift someone and help them through a difficult time in their lives.

Garwin McNeilus is a gracious Adventist Christian and a very successful businessman. Those cement and garbage trucks you follow on the highway with the name *McNeilus* on the mud flaps were his creation. When he sold the company a number of years ago, it was not only the largest firm of its kind but had something like 90 percent of the market in the U.S.

Garwin made a missionary trip to India—he was part of an evangelistic team that baptized thousands of people into Christ, becoming members of the remnant church. He saw the overwhelming poverty of India, along with millions of orphaned children walking the streets. Affluent as he is, he couldn't relieve all of the pain he witnessed. In fact, our whole nation could not solve the problems of India—we're still trying to solve ours.

But Garwin decided to do what he could. He started building orphanages, and at the time of this writing, he has built more than forty orphanages in India, each crowded with children that are being fed, educated, and led to Jesus Christ as their Savior. Garwin lit a candle instead of cursing the darkness, as the old saying goes.

Merlin Fjarli, a 3ABN board member, had a similar experience in India and has built several orphanages and churches as well. Not only can we make a difference in the world, but when we reach out to others, it makes a big difference in us.

Jesus was there to heal that man born blind. After His words, He spit on the ground, made some mud with the saliva, and put it on the man's eyes. Now, why did He do that? Not because there is any healing power in saliva—though some, like Pliny the Elder (an early church leader), thought so! He wrote a whole book on the healing qualities of saliva.

No, Christ was not proving that there is some healing power in saliva that could cure blindness. Something much deeper was involved. Christ gave the man something to do—something that would exercise his faith. He didn't just touch him and run off to the next stop on His journey. He involved the man in the process of healing. " 'Go, . . . wash in the Pool of Siloam' " (verse 7, NIV), Jesus told him.

Let's take a quick look at the pool of Siloam. The Gihon Spring is located just outside the city of Jerusalem. When Sennacherib invaded the northern kingdom of Israel, Hezekiah knew the Assyrians would be coming south to Jerusalem soon. He knew that the only chance they had to survive was to secure their water supply and bring water into the city.

They dug a tunnel in record time, digging from both directions to the middle—some 533 total yards. And they were only eleven inches off when the two tunnels met in the middle. This became known as Hezekiah's Tunnel, and it still exists and is a favorite site for the serious biblical student who travels to Jerusalem today. This tunnel brought the water from the spring into the city, at the site which came to be known as the pool of Siloam.

So it was to this pool that Christ sent this man to wash. Again, there was no special healing power in the pool of Siloam, but Jesus gave this man some specific instructions to follow. This was a demonstration of his faith. If he had ignored these instructions or chosen another place to wash, his blindness would have continued. But in trusting Jesus, he was healed.

"So the man went and washed, and came home seeing" (verse 7, NIV).

But when his neighbors saw him, a controversy erupted. At first, some of them said, "This is not the man born blind, but this man just looks like him." But the man quickly let them know that he was indeed the one who had been blind from birth—and that Jesus was the One who had healed him!

So now the issue became when the healing had taken place. Because the man was healed on the Sabbath, this created a big problem in their minds. In the Gospels, especially in the book of John, we often find Christ in conflict with the Pharisees on the matter of Sabbath observance. The command to keep the Sabbath was never in question. The day was not a problem. But, the manner in which Jesus did His healing work was another matter.

The Pharisees had participated in developing more than six hundred different regulations concerning the Sabbath that did not appear in Scripture but came from their own dictates, not from God. When Jesus broke these commands of men, they accused Him of sinning. But Christ never sinned. He was not a sinner. Sin is the transgression of the law of God, the Bible says. Christ never transgressed the law of God, but He did transgress the man-made commandments of the Pharisees!

To demonstrate some of these ridiculous rules, consider some examples. You could not place saliva even on your eyebrows or eyelashes—that would be work! You've seen a mother lick her fingers and press a wild hair on a child into place? That would be sin. Now, to actually mix it with mud was called kneading. It was also against "their" Sabbath rules—though not God's—to heal or help someone who was sick on the Sabbath. If there was an emergency, if someone was injured, you could fix him up only enough so he wouldn't die. You could not do enough that he would get well—that would be going too far. This was the kind of hairsplitting they were practicing.

Jesus came to die on the cross for our sins. But He also came to show us how to live, and He was demonstrating to us that it was lawful to do good on the Sabbath. We must never forget that Jesus had, in His preexistent state, created the world and the Sabbath, and He certainly knew how it was to be kept.

Let me share something here, for those who keep the Sabbath. You have to be careful that you don't enter into that kind of thinking. Christ was clearly showing that loading down the Sabbath with all these man-made rules wasn't what God intended. Christ was showing that the Sabbath was made for man—and not man for the Sabbath. This is to be a day of spiritual rejuvenation, not a day for trying to keep score with a whole lot of rules.

Don't take what Jesus said as a license to go out and buy and sell on God's holy day. If you do, you'll miss the whole point of what Christ was trying to give us in the blessings of the Sabbath. Take it as a day of joy and of gladness—a day when you are rejuvenated instead of a day when you go and do all the same things you did all week long. The Sabbath is a special day. They were trying to make it a day of nothing.

So why did Christ stop to heal this man? I believe that He stopped in order to raise questions. He could have said, "Stay right there. I'll be back tomorrow. I don't want to create any controversy." But He didn't. He healed the man right then, and when He did it, He violated every man-made rule.

They said, "He can't be from God, because He's a sinner." No, He wasn't a sinner.

They said, "He breaks the Sabbath." No, He never broke the Sabbath. He wrote the commandment with His very finger. It was Jesus Christ who wrote the fourth commandment. He knew the intention of the commandment.

Jesus was saying, "Listen, when I wrote the commandment, I wasn't here in person to show you how the Sabbath should be kept, but I'm here in person now, and I'm showing you that it's right and lawful to do good on the Sabbath. The Sabbath is not a day of doing nothing—it's a day of doing good." If you can possibly do something special for somebody, you want to do it on the Sabbath day.

A lady in a church I pastored went to visit in the home of a young mother who had missed church that day. When she got to that home, it was on a Sabbath afternoon, and she found the home totally in disarray. The mother had four or five children running around—little children—and she was totally out of it, just exasperated. She had lost it.

You know what this lady did? She later said, "I started right into cleaning that house up. I went in that kitchen, and I washed every dish in that kitchen, and I completely cleaned that kitchen. Then I went into the bedroom, and I made that bed and hung up those clothes. I organized that whole house. That mother was actually sane by the time I left there. Do you think, pastor, that I broke the Sabbath?"

You know what I said to her? "No! I don't think you broke the Sabbath. I think God was right there with you to help."

Now, that was not an every Sabbath event for this helpful lady. She wouldn't go out looking for housework on the Sabbath, and if you thought that, then you missed the whole point. She helped that woman back into sanity—that overwhelmed mother who had temporarily lost it. This lady was doing good on the Sabbath day. She would not have gone home and cleaned her own house on the Sabbath. She wouldn't have needed to. She had cleaned her house the day before. But she was lifting that poor mother out of a ditch of despair.

That's what Jesus Christ was there to do on that day He met the man born blind. When He did, the inquisition really started. The Pharisees began to question any witness they could find. "The Jews still did not believe that he had been blind and had received his sight until they sent for the man's parents. 'Is this your son?' they asked. 'Is this the one you say was born blind? How is it that now he can see?'

" 'We know he is our son,' the parents answered, 'and we know he was born blind. But how he can see now, or who opened his eyes, we don't know. Ask him. He is of age; he will speak for himself' " (verses 18–23, NIV).

"Check it out with him," the parents said. They were trying to avoid excommunication. There were three kinds of excommunication. First was a thirty-day expulsion. If you were expelled, you had no social contact at all. You were treated as a total outsider.

Then there was a period longer than thirty days—from thirty days up to two or three years, as the second suspension. The third and final excommunication was for life. That's when they said, "You are out of here." You couldn't even deal with them on any kind of business matters. A regular Jew wouldn't even deal with you anymore.

In Hebrew, excommunication was called "the *cherm.*" The transliteration of "the *cherm*" means "cast out." And that's what they were saying to this man who had been healed.

These religious leaders had already said that if anyone said that Jesus was the Christ, they were going to *"cherm"* him—they were going to actually de-synagogue him, get rid of him, excommunicate him.

These parents didn't want to be excommunicated. So they came to the man—and this is where I really start liking this fellow—and they asked him, "What do you think about Him? What do you have to say?"

"The man replied, 'He is a prophet.' . . . A second time they summoned the man who had been blind. 'Give glory to God,' they said. 'We know this man is a sinner' " (verses 17, 24, NIV).

"Give glory to God" was their way of saying, "You tell the truth!"

He replied, "Whether he is a sinner or not, I don't know. One thing I do know. I was blind but now I see!"

Then they asked him, "What did he do to you? How did he open your eyes?"

He answered, "I have told you already and you did not listen. Why do you want to hear it again? Do you want to become his disciples, too?"

Then they hurled insults at him and said, "You are this fellow's disciple! We are disciples of Moses! We know that God spoke to Moses, but as for this fellow, we don't even know where he comes from."

The man answered, "Now that is remarkable! You don't know where he comes from, yet he opened my eyes. We know that God does not listen to sinners. He listens to the godly man who does his will. Nobody has ever heard of opening the eyes of a man born blind. If this man were not from God, he could do nothing."

To this they replied, "You were steeped in sin at birth; how dare you lecture us!" And they threw him out (verses 25–34, NIV).

Cast out!

I can just imagine his response to them. He probably said, "Hey, look, you fellows haven't done anything for me anyway. You've always looked at me as some second-class citizen, but I was sitting along the side of that road, and a man came along, and He saw me as something else. He saw me as somebody in need. He saw me as somebody who really cared, and He reached down and touched me—He put that mud on my eyes. I did exactly what He said, and now I can see. Go ahead and throw me out."

Now, that's the Gilley version of that passage!

The Bible then says, "Jesus heard that they had thrown him out, and when he found him . . ." (verse 35, NIV). That's the story of all of us. We're lost. Jesus looked for him. The ninety and nine were safe, but there's one still out there, and He went and looked for him, didn't He? And He went and looked for this blind man and presented the gospel to him,

> . . . and when he found him, he said, "Do you believe in the Son of Man?"
>
> "Who is he, sir?" the man asked. "Tell me so that I may believe in him."
>
> Jesus said, "You have now seen him; in fact, he is the one speaking with you."
>
> Then the man said, "Lord, I believe," and he worshiped him.
>
> Jesus said, "For judgment I have come into this world, so that the blind will see and those who see will become blind."
>
> Some Pharisees who were with him heard him say this and asked, "What? Are we blind too?"
>
> Jesus said, "If you were blind, you would not be guilty of sin; but now that you claim you can see, your guilt remains" (verses 35–41, NIV).

This man first said, "Jesus was a man—and what a man!" Then he said, "He was a prophet—and what a prophet!" Then he said, "I believe this is the Son of God."

My friend, as you look at Scripture, you look at this whole story of Jesus, and you can only be impressed with what a man Jesus was—never a man spoke as did this Man. And as you look at Him even more, you see Him as a prophet—never a prophet spoke as did this Prophet.

But if you are to have life eternal, you must look at Jesus and say, "This is the Son of God, my Savior."

The blind man, healed in body and soul, said, "Now I see!"

Yes, with his physical eyes, he now saw for the first time in his life. He saw people, and homes, and streets, and animals, and the sky—and a man called Jesus.

And he said, "This is the Son of God, my Savior."

But not just his physical eyes were opened that day. For the first time in his life, he saw his own sinfulness, his own need for more than just physical healing, his desperate need to be forgiven and cleansed from the inside out.

Have your own spiritual eyes been opened yet, my reader friend—the eyes of your heart and mind and spirit? Do you see? Do you see *Him*? There before you is your Healer. Your Savior. Your Friend. Your only hope!

Chapter 10 — John 10

THE GOOD SHEPHERD

"Most assuredly, I say to you, he who does not enter the sheepfold by the door, but climbs up some other way, the same is a thief and a robber."

—*John 10:1*

When I was in the the ninth grade attending Dallas Junior Academy, we had recess at a park almost a block away. Since the day was an especially hot one, several of us were thirsty, and we ran ahead of the group back to the school building when recess was over. The principal and other teachers were behind us, walking with the other students.

We found the door locked, so we went around and climbed in a window. When our teacher—who was also the principal and a fine man—arrived to find us already in the building, he was understandably upset. We were an active, sometimes rowdy group of boys, and when he saw us, he called us "thieves and robbers."

We were indignant, of course, and quickly let him know that we were no such things! But he said he would prove it to us from the Bible, and we challenged him to do just that. So he read to us the text at the beginning of this chapter. But even though we were young and mischievous, we weren't stupid, and we quickly pointed out what Jesus really meant with this text. Perhaps he meant to make us think, or he was just overreacting—which he often did with students—but whichever it was, I have never forgotten the real meaning of this text, which is that Jesus Christ is the only way to salvation. He is the only Door.

"But he who enters by the door is the shepherd of the sheep. . . . Then Jesus said to them again, 'Most assuredly, I say to you, I am the door of the sheep' " (John 10:2, 7).

You say, "Wait a minute! Jesus says He is the Shepherd. But He also says He is the Door. How can that be?" In the Middle East, the shepherd would have what is called a sheepfold. A sheepfold was usually just a fence about four feet high, made from rocks—you can still see them out there today. Sometimes the sheepfold might be just a natural area that is backed up to a mountain, and the shepherd would add some rocks out to the front and make a little opening to the enclosed area. The sheep would go inside, and the shepherd would lie right down in that opening. So you see, the shepherd became the door! The only way to get into that sheepfold was to come over that shepherd.

Jesus says that He is the Door. And He adds, " 'The thief does not come except to steal, and to kill, and to destroy. I have come that they may have life, and that they may have it more abundantly' " (verse 10). That's exactly the reason He has come—that we might have life and have it more abundantly. Then He says, " 'I am the good shepherd; and I know My sheep, and am known by My own. As the Father knows Me, even so I know the Father; and I lay down My life for the sheep' " (verses 14, 15).

By the way, I have the full and complete conviction that Jesus is the only Shepherd. There is no other shepherd. There are porters, there are helpers, there are hirelings—but He is the only Shepherd.

As I've studied this chapter in John, I've run across books and commentaries that say that pastors too are good shepherds—maybe "undershepherds." Listen, we pastors are not shepherds, and we are not even undershepherds. I am a sheep, just as you are. Only one Shepherd exists—and that is Jesus Christ. All the rest of us are sheep. I do hope I am a sheep with a bell that helps lead other sheep to the Good Shepherd—that points lost sheep to Him. But you and I are still sheep, and He is the only Shepherd.

Now, after reading through the first twenty-one verses of chapter 10, we come to a place where there's an interval of two months' time between verse 21 and these words in verse 22, "Now it was the Feast of Dedication in Jerusalem, and it was winter." Yes, it was winter. "And Jesus walked in the temple, in Solomon's porch" (verse 23). Winter weather over in Israel and Jerusalem is quite unpredictable. It can be very cold—or you can have a beautiful warm day. Or you can have a day when it is cold and wet. If you go there during the winter, you want to take a coat, but you could end up with beautiful warm days and cold nights. Even in the summer in Jerusalem, it can get cold at night.

The scene depicted here takes place with Jesus being at Solomon's porch. He's attending the Feast of Dedication—also called the Feast of Lights. To explain why it's called the Feast of Lights, I'll need to sketch in a little background here.

About 175 B.C., a man by the name of Antiochus Epiphanes, from Assyria, took over Israel. This man was Hellenistic—a word that has to do with the principles and culture of Greek civilization. And anything the Greeks ever did, Antiochus thought was great.

Antiochus wanted to eradicate the Jewish religion and the Jewish way of life and replace it with Greek religion and culture. The leaders basically went along with him. However, he couldn't get everybody else to go along with him. He tried at first by bringing in some easy measures, but finally he moved in and attacked Jerusalem. He killed eighty thousand Jews and sold into slavery around the world an equal number of Jews.

Then Antiochus went to the temple, and—imagine this—he turned that temple into a pagan temple, sacrificing pigs to pagan gods on the altar. Can you imagine anything that would be more defiling to a Jew than for a pig to be sacrificed in the temple? They also turned the temple into a house of prostitution, as this was a part of their worship.

A young man named Judas Maccabeus, whose father was a Jewish priest, left Jerusalem, traveled north, and organized a band of guerilla fighters. They began to fight hard against Antiochus, and finally, in 164 B.C., they threw off the oppression of Antiochus Epiphanes and celebrated the Feast of Dedication, in which they rededicated the temple. They called this the Feast of Lights. And since that time the Jewish people have celebrated this Feast, which is now called Hanukkah.

So Jesus was there for the Feast of Lights, or Hanukkah. "Then the Jews surrounded Him and said to Him, 'How long do You keep us in doubt? If You are the Christ, tell us plainly' " (verse 24). Now, in the book of John, several times prior, Jesus had already told the people plainly that He was the Christ. Nonetheless, they are asking Him again. They keep asking the right question, but they never accept the answer they receive. If He says, "Yes, I am the Christ," then they want to stone Him for saying so. "Jesus answered them, 'I told you, and you do not believe. The works that I do in My Father's name, they bear witness of Me' " (verse 25).

Now why are they asking Jesus, particularly at this time, if He's the Christ? Because right now, at the Feast of Dedication—the Feast of Lights, Hanukkah—they are thinking about what Judas Maccabeus had done and that they would be put back under oppression. Not as bad as it was back then, yet still oppression. Rome is in control.

So they are standing there thinking to themselves, *Let's see if we can goad Him into doing something. Maybe He'll lead a rebellion like the one Judas did—or then again, maybe He'll say something, and these Romans will put Him to death for what He says.* So they asked their question, but not because they really wanted to know the answer. They weren't serious about their question. They simply wanted to create a situation that would either give them the right to stone Him or that would incite the Romans to put Him to death.

Then Jesus answers, and sure enough, when He does, they pick up the rocks to stone Him. In that part of the world, believe me, there's never a shortage of rocks. You can see why stoning was the popular way to put people to death. You didn't have to send somebody out to find stones. They are always handy.

If you notice the newscasts, even Palestinian youth today, when they are antagonizing Israeli soldiers, what are they doing? They are throwing rocks at them. There's just no way that all the rocks over there are ever going to be picked up, I guarantee you.

Have you ever looked around in most American cities? You look around for a rock to throw, and you can't find a good rock. If you are a rock thrower, you need to move to Israel, where you would be in paradise! I've been there many times, and one person who made many trips with me was my good friend Dr. Carl Markstrom. His wife, Norma, also made several trips, but later on she would tell him to go on "to that pile of rocks"—her pet name for Israel—without her.

Now we come to verses which I believe are some of the most— if not the most—beautiful in all of Scripture. " 'My sheep hear My voice, and I know them, and they follow Me. And I give them eternal life, and they shall never perish; neither shall anyone snatch them out of My hand' " (verses 27, 28).

We read these words and rush by, not realizing that the greatest truth in all of Scripture is located right here! " 'My Father, who has given them to Me, is greater than all; and no one is able to snatch them out of My Father's hand. I and My Father are one' " (verses 29, 30).

Jesus is saying that He's God—and He's also saying that if you believe in Him, then you are His sheep! " 'But you do not believe, because you are not of My sheep, as I said to you. My sheep hear My voice, and I know them, and they follow Me' " (verses 26, 27). The difference between being His sheep and not being His sheep is believing. And if you believe in Him, my friend, He says you have life eternal and that no one and no power can take you out of His hand. That's exciting to me.

So many today are anxious and insecure—especially about whether or not they can or will be saved. But all anxiety and insecurity can be healed simply by believing in Jesus as the Good Shepherd—by resting in the certainty of His salvation. And it's not because of who we are, not because of what we've done, or because of something good in us. It's because of His saving power as our Good Shepherd.

Let's say that we know a man named Shep, who is a shepherd with a hundred sheep. A few weeks go by, and we come back to visit with Shep. "How many sheep do you have now, Shep?" We're thinking that with new lambs being born, the flock must have grown.

"I have about thirty-five sheep left."

"Where did you lose the other sixty-five sheep?" we ask.

"Oh, I don't know," he replies, "just here and there."

Is Shep a good shepherd? Of course not! A good shepherd doesn't lose his sheep, does he? Christ says, "I am the Good Shepherd." And He tells the story of the man who left the ninety and nine sheep and went out and got the one that was lost.

If you have accepted Jesus Christ as your Lord and Savior, then you are His sheep. You are His sheep—and He cares for you. And He has done something else. He has pledged to save you—eternally save you.

We always want to add a whole lot of other things to this. We always want to say, "But there's something that I have to do." Yes, there is. You need to simply *believe* in Him. People say, "Ah, but that's so easy." Well, is it? No, it's the most difficult thing in the world.

But for some reason, we would rather have a list. If somebody can just give me a list and tell me to dress this way, walk this way, talk this way, and act this way, then I'll know how to be saved. Listen to me now. If we have any list, there should be only one thing on that list: *believe in Jesus as my Savior*. Trust in Him as your Good Shepherd.

Can you do anything to lose your salvation? Of course. If you choose to leave Him, He's not going to drag you kicking and screaming into heaven. But when you believe in Him and trust in Him and invite Him into your life, He will bring about changes in your heart that you could never bring about yourself. Please believe this, because not only is it true, it's the key to you living eternally.

If you do this, things you once loved, you will start to hate, and places you used to go and things you used to do will no longer hold any desire for you. If you find that they do, it is because you have not continued to give Him your love and trust. You have not continued to eat the Bread of Life and have stopped drinking from the Spring of Living Water.

Jesus never takes away our free will, but He has chosen you and called you to eternal life. And you can have complete assurance of it right now. You can have it because Jesus teaches it and offers it. This is not some "new theology." These are the words of Jesus Christ Himself, right here in John, the tenth chapter. This is not some theologian presenting some flowery, fancy idea—this is what Jesus Himself says to you.

Today, would you do something? Would you stop trying to save yourself and let Jesus be your Shepherd? Would you accept Him as your Savior, if you have never really done that? Would you choose to believe in Him? Would you trust Him 100 percent?

George Vandeman often said, "You know, when I look at myself, I don't know how I can be saved, but when I look at Jesus, I don't know how I could be lost." Let me tell you something: if you give yourself to Him and you trust in Him, *you will not be lost.*

And I hope there's not anyone who would say, "I can just give myself to Him and go right on sinning and living as I please." That would not be giving yourself to Him, would it? We know what Paul, in Romans, says about that. If you really love Him and are giving yourself to Him, you're not going to turn around and go off in rebellion against Him—absolutely not!

But on the other hand, even if, after giving your life to Jesus your Shepherd, you may make mistakes in your human weakness, that doesn't take you out of the fold. You're still in the hands of Jesus. There were ninety and nine that safely lay in the shelter of the fold, but one was out on the hill far away.

I am so thankful for a Shepherd who saves 100 percent of those who come to Him. He not only saves the ninety and nine, but He saves the one. He goes out and gets that one and saves him, because He brings *all* the sheep home. He's the Good Shepherd. He would give His life for you. He *has* given His life for you!

You may be just one sheep, but while Jesus died for all His sheep, He also died just for you. Just for you alone. Who else has ever loved you that much? Who else ever will?

Chapter 11 — John 11:35

THE SIN THAT BREAKS GOD'S HEART

They should have known that it was not too late for Lazarus—but they doubted. Jesus could not have been crying from feeling sorry for Lazarus, because He knew that He was soon to raise Lazarus to life again.

Then we shift to another scene. We look at the disciples out on a stormy sea, with Jesus asleep in the bottom of the boat. When the storm unleashed its full fury, they cried out to Him, "Lord, have You no concern at all? Do You not even care if we perish?" I believe that made Jesus very sad. I believe it may even have brought Him to tears. How could they think that He didn't care—that He didn't love them?

In this chapter, I want to consider a sin that breaks the very heart of God. And that sin is simply this—*to doubt His love for us*! You know, sometimes people even believe that it is intellectually stimulating to doubt. And I am amazed in classes where it seems that the teacher's whole aim is to introduce doubt. So for twenty-seven minutes of the class, students are bombarded with doubt. Then in the last two or three minutes, the teacher tries to rectify the damage done and minimize the doubt. I believe that is a satanic method of teaching—and I don't believe we should use it. I really don't.

You see, I've seen people leave a class like that after fifteen minutes. They weren't there for the last three minutes. They weren't there when the teacher tried to put things together again after breaking everything into pieces. An approach like that may be OK if you are dealing with geometry. It may be OK if you are dealing with mathematics. It may be OK if you are dealing with history. But it is not OK when you are dealing with spiritual things.

Never break down, never introduce doubt, never question God. Yet we have, haven't we? And we all have—not just teachers. And I believe it makes Christ cry—that it makes His heart heavy when we question what He has done for us. How can He not be grieved when we, His own children, live and talk and act as if He had left us to our own designs?

My friend, when we start to focus on the circumstances of life rather than on the Lord, that is when doubt takes over. Looking at the problem instead of the solution—which is Jesus Christ—is how doubt gains control. Today we stand on a higher mountain than any before us have ever stood upon. We have nineteen hundred years of testimony about Jesus Christ and His ministry. We have a completed Bible, and we have the Spirit of Prophecy with all of its beauty. We stand in—and are judged by—a greater light than has shone on any other generation. We see the fullness of the love of God and what He has done for and through us.

My friend, for every moment of every day, we should always trust in Jesus. But still, with all of this—with all the testimony of what He's done for us—still, too often we doubt His love. Still, we doubt that He will hear our cry. Still, we doubt that He will do for us what is right for us.

For a moment, let's consider Joseph. A number of years ago, I worked on a doctor of divinity degree by distance learning, where I could study at my own pace, and I eventually finished. In one of the courses, a professor presented five hundred comparisons between Joseph and Jesus—those comparisons amazed me. As a young man, the story of Joseph was my favorite in all the Bible.

I don't know about you, but when Joseph and his brothers were finally reconciled together, it brought up within me deep emotions. I wanted to weep. What a beautiful thing it was to read of how kindly and gently he dealt with his brothers! It is amazing how much trouble these brothers got into simply because they doubted their father's love for them.

They looked at Joseph, and somehow they thought, *Our father loves him better—he cares more for Joseph than for us.* They should have rejoiced that the two had such a fantastic father-son relationship. But they didn't.

How many times children become jealous of the relationship a brother or sister has with Mom or Dad. I had a brother who had a very close relationship with my father, and for many years, some used to say that Dad was partial to him. And only in recent times have I come to understand that this wasn't the case. Actually, my brother was partial to my dad, and he loved him so much that my dad could only respond. The real problem was not that Dad loved him too much but that we stood back and did not show our love for Dad as my brother did. It was not my brother's problem, and it was not Dad's problem—it was our problem.

Joseph loved his father, but instead of his brothers seeing that as what could be their own relationship with their father, they began to doubt that the father really loved them. When we start doubting the love of the Father, something happens to us— something truly terrible happens to us. Have you ever envied someone else's spiritual relationship with the heavenly Father? Have you ever looked at somebody and asked yourself, *Why is it that their prayers are always answered? Why does it seem that they are never unloved, that they are never lonely, that they are never unneeded? Why is that?*

Have you ever thought this way? It is dangerous ground. We may question whether the Father loves us as much as He loves someone else. We may ask ourselves, *Where is the evidence of His love? Where's the evidence that He is working in my life?* But when we begin to doubt His love for us, it opens up a flood-gate.

Now these men—these brothers of Joseph—were kings out of Jacob's loins. They were a chosen generation—chosen men. They had been with their father at Bethel when he built an altar to God. They had been in his presence and witnessed his sacrifice. They had been to Shechem and buried their idols there under the oak tree. They had changed their garments for new garments representing robes of righteousness. But here they were now, thinking they were not equal with their brother in their father's love, and ugliness and hatred came into their experience.

When we question our Father's love, one of the first things that starts to happen is that our speech begins to change. We become hard and mean and critical. You remember that when Peter denied the Lord, what did they say? " '[His] speech betrayeth [him]' " (Matthew 26:73, KJ21). And the speech of Joseph's brothers began to betray them. They sold their brother into slavery.

They stood out there as if they were slave auctioneers, and they argued and haggled with those Ishmaelites. Finally, they sold Joseph their brother for twenty pieces of silver. And to show how sin hardens the heart, after they sold him off into slavery, they just went back to keeping their sheep as if nothing had happened. And for twenty long, hard years, their father grieved—and all those years, they never had the decency to confess to him their sin and tell him what they had done. They hardened their hearts. Why? Because they doubted their father's love for them.

You know, Israel did exactly the same thing. Let me show it to you in the book of Malachi. You probably think the only time we preachers ever mention Malachi is to talk about tithing, right? But there's another important message early on in Malachi. " 'I have loved you,' says the LORD. / 'Yet you say, / "In what way have You loved us?" ' " (Malachi 1:2). After all that God had done for them, Israel could still ask, "In what way have You loved us?" Amazing!

Sometimes our whole message seems to be—what? Our favorite song seems to be "Fill My Cup, Lord." Fill me up. Let me tell you something: being in a relationship with God isn't all "Give me, give me, give me." It's also "What can I do for You, Lord?" When God begins hearing that question from us, then suddenly the filling up comes without our begging for it.

When we doubt God's love and question it—virtually demanding proof of it, as Israel did—we are denying the greatest gift of His love, the gift of His Son Jesus Christ on the cross. What more could He do? The greatest all-time demonstration of His love for you and me is that He gave His Son.

Now, the amazing thing here is that not even their sinful doubts kept God from loving these men. He brought about a hunger in them—a famine. You know, sometimes we have to feel a hunger for spiritual things before we really begin to look for them, don't we? Sometimes we have to hit upon hard times before we really begin to hunger for God and want to know Him.

And those men had a famine—they were starving both physically and spiritually. They went to Egypt for corn, and the Bible tells me in Genesis that Joseph—now second in Egypt only to Pharaoh—recognized his brothers, but they did not recognize him. There's a message right there, isn't there? God recognizes us, but sometimes we don't recognize Him.

Then Joseph put his brothers through a trial. Now, when I used to read this as a younger man, I looked at it and said, "Aha! Joseph is getting back at his brothers now, isn't he?" I've since repented that I ever even thought that, because that's not what Joseph was doing at all. I once thought he was getting some revenge here—that he was working his brothers over a little bit. But no, that wasn't it at all.

If you really look at Joseph's heart, you see the tenderness there and not an ounce of revenge. Instead, Joseph was testing them, trying to find out how their hearts were now toward God, toward their father, and toward their brother Benjamin. He was testing them on that point only. This is one of the greatest stories of grace you will ever find. You see, these brothers needed to confront their own guilt and shame. They needed to come to the end of themselves before God could do something for them.

And that's exactly where we too have to come. We have to come to a place where we know that there is nothing good in us—that we cannot save ourselves but that we are saved only by what Jesus Christ did at the cross. Jesus may be doing some wonderful things in your life right now, and I pray that He is. And I believe in spiritual growth. But you are not saved by what Jesus is doing in your life. You are not saved by how much you've grown spiritually. You are saved by what Jesus did on the cross—and don't ever forget it. Of course, by believing in what Jesus did on the cross and by trusting Him fully, growth in your life will begin to happen.

The brothers came to the place where they felt their guilt. "Then they said to one another [because they didn't think Joseph could understand them], 'We are truly guilty concerning our brother, for we saw the anguish of his soul when he pleaded with us, and we would not hear; therefore this distress has come upon us' " (Genesis 42:21).

I don't know if there was something about Joseph that reminded them of their long-lost brother or what, but suddenly all that guilt came back upon them. They truly thought they were going to be judged. And you know something? When we are guilty—when we doubt God's love—all we really expect is judgment.

"Lord, what have I done? My sin—I know that's why my family is falling apart. My sin—that's why this is happening to me." And we expect judgment, because we do not understand the real truth and love of God.

What did Joseph say to his brothers? First of all, you see that his heart is broken. Verse 24 says that he turned away from them and wept. His heart was full of love for his brothers, and he wept. And he said to them, "Come and dine."

When Peter denied the Lord, he cursed, he swore, he denied Him. After the cross, the next time Peter saw Him, Jesus was standing on the shore of the Sea of Galilee cooking fish. And what did He say to Peter? He didn't say, "Oh, there you are—the one who denied Me." No. He said to Peter what Joseph said to his brothers: "Come and dine with Me."

We look at Joseph here with his brothers. The Bible says that they sat in one place, and he sat in another. They were in the same place, but there was no real fellowship happening yet. Sometimes we too are in the place of God's house, but there's no real fellowship—we are not really dining with Him.

As we look at this scene of Joseph and his brothers, we see the real illustration of grace—unmerited love. That's what grace is. They didn't deserve it, and we don't deserve it either. God simply extends it to us.

As the brothers sat there, they had a good time together. They began to loosen up and enjoy their time with each other. Now, as you will remember, the revelation of who Joseph really was didn't come through to them when they were there having a good time together, did it? It came to them later when they were brokenhearted—when they were contrite men and their spirit was broken. Joseph sent them back—but had his royal cup put into Benjamin's sack.

When they started for home, Joseph sent his steward after them. When the steward caught up with them, of course he found the cup in Benjamin's sack. They knew this meant Benjamin's death and their own lifetime of servanthood. After all the promises they had made to their father to care for Benjamin, the Bible says they now fell on their faces. They rent their clothes and fell before Joseph, broken and contrite. Joseph told all the others to leave—to clear the room. What came next was to be only between Joseph and his brothers.

You remember that when Jesus was there with the woman caught in adultery, many were standing around, and what did Jesus do? He began to write their sins in the dust and cleared them all out, till only the woman and Jesus remained. Joseph clears out that room except for his brothers, and then he begins to cry. The Egyptians could hear him throughout the entire palace. Finally, Joseph said to his brothers, "I am Joseph. I am your brother!"

They were frightened. Why? Because they didn't know his heart yet. They were frightened because they thought he would take revenge. He had every possible chance to take his revenge, but the brothers still didn't understand his heart—a heart of love and compassion.

The English preacher T. Austin-Sparks made a statement that I felt is worthy of quotation. He said, "God will allow crises to be created in our lives, out of which information will not extract us, but only a revelation of grace." We often seem to think that if only we have enough knowledge—enough information—we can get out of anything. But that can only happen with a revelation of grace. No way out is available, except through God.

These men now on their faces before Joseph have no way out except through his mercy. And suddenly, they realize that mercy is exactly what they are going to get. Jacob the patriarch came down, and they were all reunited. You know, it would be a beautiful thing if this were the end of the story.

We usually stop the story there. But the amazing thing is that after Jacob died, what did the brothers say—*again*? When Joseph's brothers saw that their father was dead, they said, " 'Perhaps Joseph will hate us, and may actually repay us for all the evil which we did to him' " (Genesis 50:15). Here again, we find an example of how those who should easily have been able to trust someone's love, instead doubted it.

I'm convinced that unless we have a vision of God's love and understand His love for us—but more than that, trust His love for us—we will never be able to stand through the things about to come on the earth. We never will.

As a young preacher, I felt that to get people ready for the time of trouble I had to talk about all the things that are going to come upon the earth. Well, we've seen a lot of things come along already, and there are a lot more things coming. And I don't think it does one bit of good to dwell entirely on those things. What we most need is to develop a heart of love and trust that we will be able to stand whatever comes—even the day-to-day pressures of life. For some, there could be no future time of trouble any worse than what they have already gone through. Preparation, by learning to trust God's love for us, is what is most important.

We have to come to the place, my friend, where we would much rather die physically than to even think of dying spiritually. Jesus asked if, when the Son of man came, He would find faith on the earth. He was asking if He would find anyone who really trusted Him—who really trusts God's love.

When all things break loose on this earth, it might not be easy then to learn how to trust that God loves you and will see you through. But that's when you will most need to hold on to Him and trust in His love.

Back when I was about ten years old, I came to a place where I didn't think my father loved me. I always felt my mother loved me, but not my father. He was a strong disciplinarian, and I didn't think he loved me at all. I had two friends, one of whose father hardly ever came home. He felt as if he had no reason to go home. So the three of us decided we were going to run away from home. After all, we had bicycles.

Now, I have usually been able to plan things pretty well, so I planned our runaway right down to a T. The best time to do it was Sabbath morning. You know, if you don't go to school, they will catch you right away—they're looking for you. But Sabbath

mornings we always went to the church and handed out literature in the morning, because we had church in the afternoon.
Our pastor was somewhere else on Sabbath morning and we
thought that would be a good day to get started.

So I got up that morning just as if I were going out to pass out
literature. I had my sleeping bag already tied on the bike, out
around the back of the house, and a few provisions. I had some
money—maybe ten or twelve dollars. We were all ready.

I met my friends at the rendezvous point, and we started up
the road. Right from the first, we thought the cops were looking
for us, so every time we saw a policeman, we would hide. That's
guilt, isn't it? About noon, our families finally realized something
was wrong. They didn't know where we were, and finally, my
younger brother—who had been sworn to secrecy—went ahead
and told my parents that yes, he's left home—he's gone. Then
the cops did start looking for us.

We traveled about seventeen miles away from home, spending a lot of time under bridges—hiding here and there now and
then. One of my friends had read that west of Fort Worth were
ranches where you could get a job. So we were going out there to
get ourselves a job on a ranch—at ten years of age, a fairly early
start in life!

Then they caught us. My dad came in the pickup truck and
threw the bikes in the back. And we got in the truck and rode
home. Not much was said. But when we got home, Dad called
me into the back room and asked, "Son, why did you leave?"

"I don't feel that anybody cares whether I'm here or not," I
replied.

I looked at my dad—he was a pretty good-sized man, thin
but tall—and he was looking at me as tears came to his eyes.

"Son," he said, "I love you." And I realized that he really did
love me.

Now the other two boys had gone home. One of the fathers
didn't even know his son had been gone all day. My other friend's

mother and father got into a fight on whether to discipline him or not—and there was no discipline at all. No such luck for me, though. My father took off his belt and applied it the way he knew how, but afterward he reached down and hugged me to him. I knew he loved me.

Only perhaps a couple of times after that was I tempted to question my father's love. I remember that it put him through a great strain whenever he thought I questioned his love.

Later, when I was in college, word came that my dad had cancer. He was only fifty-eight years old, and I went home to see him during one of the breaks. My dad was not a very emotional person. Whenever we left each other, he would usually just say, "We'll see you later." But as I left him that time to go back to school, I reached the car, and suddenly we both turned and began hugging each other. He hugged me so hard even in his illness, that I knew beyond question that my father loved me.

I don't know just where you are at this moment in your walk with God. I don't know how much you may struggle sometimes with doubts as to whether or not He loves you. You may have missed a father's love. You may have missed a mother's love. You may never have felt loved by your brother or your sister, but I want to assure you right now that God loves you. He loves you no matter what. He loves you with no strings attached. Nothing you can ever do will make Him stop loving you.

You may make mistakes. But who doesn't? You may do things you should never do in life. You may be far from the person you want to be. But whatever you do, I want to challenge you to never again doubt God's love for you.

God created you. In Jesus, He lived for you. He died for you. He gives you life each new day. He forgives you. He accepts you back when you run away from Him. He thinks of you constantly. He promises you His help, His gifts, His companionship—and everything you could possibly need to be truly happy in this life.

How can you—how can I—how can any of us doubt that kind of lavish, stubborn love?

Chapter 12 — John 12

LAVISH LOVE

Then, six days before the Passover, Jesus came to Bethany, where Lazarus was who had been dead, whom He had raised from the dead.

—*John 12:1*

Hope, Arkansas, is a little town known as the birthplace of former president Bill Clinton. Except for that, it would be just another of ten thousand other small and not very well-known towns.

And here in John 12, we find another little town mentioned that wasn't really well known till something amazing happened there. Because no one really heard much of Bethany till the name Lazarus became known far and wide. Bethany—a suburb of Jerusalem two miles outside the city—became known as the town where Lazarus lived—but far more, as the town where Lazarus was raised from the dead.

As this chapter opens, a feast is taking place in Bethany. Perhaps it was at the home of Mary, Martha, and Lazarus. But there's also some evidence it may have been at the home of Simon the leper. Martha, one of the two sisters of Lazarus, was serving. Now let me tell you something about Martha. She was *always* serving.

I don't care what the occasion, if she was present, she was serving. You maybe know people like that, too. You go to their place, and they are scurrying around tending to everyone's needs. Or they come to your house, and they go right into the kitchen and start helping, don't they?

We love to have people like that come over. I mean, even after the meal is finished, they don't stop until the dishes are done. They don't say, "Let's just let them set aside, and we'll visit." No. Certain people really do get a lot of joy out of serving.

That's really the whole message of Christianity—service. The idea of Christianity is that we serve each other. The whole idea of the Lord's Supper—and of footwashing in particular—is to serve one another. Today, though, the concept of serving yourself has taken hold. Even when you go fill up with gas. "Serve yourself." Have you ever gone to the gas pump and filled your car, then pulled it aside and said, "Now I'm going to serve ten other people. The next ten people who drive up, I'm going to fill their tank?"

They would probably lock you up, wouldn't they? They would say, "There is some idiot out there trying to fill everybody's tank. Call the police." Why? Because we are in a self-serve economy, a self-serve world. Serve yourself. Be self-sufficient. Take care of yourself. Self is number one.

That is the antithesis of Christianity. You see, we should all be serving one another. The concept works, too. It is Christ's concept. Self-serve is not the way of Christianity. Over and over the message of Jesus is that we haven't come to be served but to serve. We haven't come to be number one—to be lifted up, to be a big shot—but to serve and to help. Too often, we forget that.

Unfortunately, today, even in Christianity, we've gotten the star concept. We should be getting away from that—the idea that we lift people up and push them up and make a "Christian celebrity" out of them. It's not right. It's just not the way it should be.

At this feast, those who came were there to celebrate the resurrection of Lazarus. He had been dead, but now he was alive. I would love to go to a celebration like that, wouldn't you? And one of these days, at the Second Coming, we'll have a celebration of those resurrected from the dead. So we'll each get our chance at a celebration similar to this one they held for Lazarus.

They may also have been celebrating the healing of Simon the leper from his disease—another miracle Jesus had recently performed. So they are having a supper in honor of Jesus—the Healer, the Resurrection, and the Life. Now if you actually look at when this celebration took place, it was probably on a Saturday night. Because the next day, according to the Gospel writers, Christ's triumphal entry into Jerusalem took place, on the day we call Palm Sunday.

Typical of a celebration or feast in a Jewish home, then, the bread had been prepared the day before. So it was not a big effort to put on a feast. Everyone just brings along their salads and cold dishes, and then after sunset, perhaps a fire was built to warm up some of the other dishes. For sure, though, no cooking would have taken place during the Sabbath hours at all—not in any Jewish home.

Often, my family and I have been in Jerusalem on the Sabbath. More than once while there, we've gone on a beautiful sunny Sabbath day to a place such as the Garden Tomb. One year, we went to the Garden Tomb, and Elder M. D. Lewis put on the high priest's robe. This particular Sabbath was sunny but chilly, so we found an area near the Tomb with a lot of sun and shared a beautiful service there. Elder Lewis wore the robe and explained its meaning and how it related to the ministry of Jesus.

Then we did some other things around Jerusalem that day, and when evening came, we had a little something to eat. We went down to Ben Yehuda Street in the Israeli sector of Jerusalem. The streets were virtually empty. In the Jewish sector, no one was out—the people were inside their homes. Over in the Arab sector, it was business as usual. The day before, Friday, had been their quiet day.

Then the sun set, and one hour later, suddenly, almost like an army, we looked up and saw people pouring into the streets—young people, older people, people with families, people pushing carts and little baby buggies. Families were coming, and they were all heading down to the Ben Yehuda Street section. Shops were opening, and a party atmosphere seemed to spread through the area. On other nights, this area was fairly active, but nothing like on Saturday night. We saw wall to wall people!

So after the sun is set, I see this special supper in the honor of our Lord. Mary and Martha are there, and Martha is serving. Mary, on the other hand, is intent on one thing—honoring Jesus. She has brought with her an expensive perfumed oil. For Jesus, Mary has what we might call extravagant love. Nothing is too good for Jesus, and she is determined to give Him the best she can afford. It also seems that Mary is so intent on what she intends to do that she is totally oblivious to the presence of anyone else in the room. She not only doesn't care that they are there, she doesn't even see them—she sees only Jesus.

Mary anoints Jesus with the oil. She bends to Jesus' feet. The love of humility. The humility of love. She bathes His feet with this fine-smelling perfume, and suddenly, its scent filled the room. If people hadn't noticed Mary before, they certainly know she is there now. What is that aroma? What's going on?

This was probably the last real opportunity she would have to do this for Jesus. When the disciple Judas complained that Mary was wasting this expensive perfume, you remember what Jesus said: " 'Let her alone; she has kept this for the day of My burial' " (John 12:7). And that would be very soon. This was Saturday night, and by the next Friday, Jesus would be placed in the tomb.

You know, sometimes you just have to seize the opportunity,

don't you? Mary was seizing the opportunity to say, "Thank You, Lord, for bringing my brother back to life. Thank You for being my Savior and my Lord and my God—and I want to honor You." Sometimes we let opportunities pass.

Thomas Carlyle, a great man, was married to his wife, Jane. When she died, Carlyle deeply regretted that he had not told his wife properly how much he loved her. In personality, he was distant and quite standoffish, and he sometimes had the attitude that said, "If I didn't love you, I'd tell you." Sometimes, gentlemen, maybe we too have that attitude, and we need to take the opportunity to let people know we care for them. Mary took the chance—she took the opportunity.

Now I want us to look more closely at Judas. We see this great contrast. Three and a half years Mary had been close to Jesus—and so had Judas. In fact, Judas had been with Him even more than Mary. Every place Jesus went, Judas was along. Yet we see such a different reaction from the two of them. Mary was all about extravagant love—nothing could be too good for her Lord. But Judas was an embittered man. He was torn apart by ambition. He wanted to be something—to be somebody. He wanted his Lord to take over control and restore Israel to power, yes. But he was even more interested in himself, and he was bitter and critical. Bitterness and criticism seem to travel together.

So Judas had the same experience, the same opportunities as Mary—he's been with Christ all this time, yet he reacts differently. He even reacts differently than the other eleven. The Bible tells us that he criticizes: " 'Why was this fragrant oil not sold for three hundred denarii and given to the poor?' This he said, not that he cared for the poor, but because he was a thief, and had the money box; and he used to take what was put in it" (verses 5, 6).

Now, even though back in John, the sixth chapter, Jesus says that one of His disciples is a devil, Jesus still trusted Judas with the money. He loved him enough to allow Judas to be tested in the place of his most severe temptation. And if in that place Judas had crucified self, his life might have gone in a totally different direction. But he gave in to that temptation, that weakness for money. It so often happens that when someone is placed at the point of their weakness, that if they do not choose God's strength and gain victory, they instead become weaker and weaker.

A man worked for me one time, and I trusted him completely. In fact, I trusted everybody in our firm. We had a beautiful spirit of trust together. Nearly everybody had a key, including this man. But he stole from my business. He didn't just steal a little—he stole a lot. Amazingly, when finally it was uncovered, and I confronted him, he said, "It is your fault."

"It is my fault?" I said. "Because I trusted you, it is my fault?"

"Yes," he said, "you made it too easy. You made it so easy I couldn't resist."

Jesus made it easy for Judas, too, didn't He? He said, "Here, you carry the money—you take care of the money." Jesus could have given it to anybody else, but He knew the heart of Judas. He knew the selfishness there, and Jesus gave him the chance to choose a better way. But Judas rejected that chance. What a contrast in how these two people—Judas and Mary—related to Jesus. One had a heart like stone—the heart of the other was soft and full of love.

" 'He who loves his life will lose it, and he who hates his life in this world will keep it for eternal life' " (verse 25). The difference between Mary and Judas was that Mary really hated her own life in this world, and hers was a movement of humility when she went to Jesus' feet. Judas loved his life—he loved it to the point he would do anything he could to better himself—but instead, he lost it. " 'If anyone serves Me, let him follow Me; and where I am, there My servant will be also. If anyone serves Me, him My Father will honor' " (verse 26). " 'And I, if I am lifted up from the earth, will draw all peoples to Myself' " (verse 32).

The next day after the celebration in Bethany, the Bible says, a great multitude came to an even greater feast—the celebration of Passover—in Jerusalem. I've read estimates of as many as 256,000 lambs slain at one Passover, with maybe 2.7 million people in attendance. I don't have any question that those figures are quite accurate. The crowds spill out from Jerusalem all over the countryside—even out to Bethany. But now they are headed back to the temple area.

You remember the story of what happened that day. Jesus said, "Go to this certain place, and tell them a donkey is tied there. And if anybody says anything to you, just say that the Lord has need of it."

Jesus got on the donkey and rode it into Jerusalem. It's been called the Triumphal Entry—and in a way, it was truly a wonderful event. But in a way, it was also very sad, because these same people crying out their praises would within days be crying out "Crucify Him!" Soon enough, they concluded that Jesus wasn't really the great deliverer, come to free them from Roman oppression—and they turn on Him.

But today, he is the King. He is the Messiah. After all, just look at what He did in Bethany. He raised the dead. They began to shout and sing their praises and hosannas, some taken from Psalms 113–118.

> "Fear not, daughter of Zion;
> Behold, your King is coming,
> Sitting on a donkey's colt" (verse 15).

"His disciples did not understand these things at first; but when Jesus was glorified, then they remembered that these things were written about Him and that they had done these things to Him" (verse 16).

What was happening there as Jesus entered Jerusalem reflected two great Bible confirmations that He was indeed the Messiah. First, His entry into Jerusalem was a fulfillment of Bible prophecy.

All the way back in the book of Genesis, it was prophesied that the Messiah would arrive on a colt, a donkey. The book of Zechariah promised the same thing. And in Daniel, the exact time of the Messiah's arrival was predicted—and Jesus arrived precisely on time. No one else came along at the right time, in the right way, and fulfilled to the letter every Bible prophecy of the Messiah.

The other great Bible confirmation that Jesus was the Messiah were the miracles He performed. And miracles marked the entire ministry of Jesus: the feeding of the five thousand, healing the sick, raising the dead. "Therefore the people, who were with Him when He called Lazarus out of his tomb and raised him from the dead, bore witness. For this reason the people also met Him, because they heard that He had done this sign. The Pharisees therefore said among themselves, 'You see that you are accomplishing nothing. Look, the world has gone after Him!' " (verses 17–19).

And the world had indeed gone after Him. The Pharisees were whipped. They were defeated because, for one thing, they had gone after Him for the wrong reasons. They had misunderstood what the Messiah came to do. They had studied the prophecies of Daniel. They read about the four kingdoms, and they knew Rome was the fourth kingdom Daniel saw in vision. And they also knew that after Rome would come a kingdom that would endure forever. They had no doubt that they would be that final kingdom—and that the Messiah would be their Deliverer and Ruler. They looked for a military Messiah who would overthrow the Romans and take control.

Then Jesus began to speak, and He began to say things such as, " 'The hour has come that the Son of Man should be glorified. Most assuredly, I say to you, unless a grain of wheat falls into the ground and dies, it remains alone; but if it dies, it produces much grain' " (verses 23, 24). If it dies? They didn't understand this.

And then He said,

"Father, glorify Your name." Then a voice came from heaven, saying, "I have both glorified it and will glorify it again."

Therefore the people who stood by and heard it said that it had thundered. Others said, "An angel has spoken to Him."

Jesus answered and said, "This voice did not come because of Me, but for your sake. Now is the judgment of this world; now the ruler of this world will be cast out. And I, if I am lifted up from the earth, will draw all peoples to Myself." This He said, signifying by what death He would die (verses 28–33).

The people seemed confused.

" 'We have heard from the law that the Christ remains forever; and how can You say, "The Son of Man must be lifted up"? Who is this Son of Man?' " (verse 34). "If You are going to be the Christ," they were telling Him, "You are supposed to come and set up Your kingdom, and You are supposed to set it up so that we as Israel can now be the ruling kingdom of the earth forever. We know about the Messiah who will rule forever, but who is this Son of Man?"

"Then Jesus said to them, 'A little while longer the light is with you. Walk while you have the light, lest darkness overtake you; he who walks in darkness does not know where he is going. While you have the light, believe in the light, that you may become sons of light.' These things Jesus spoke, and departed, and was hidden from them" (verses 35, 36).

Amazing, isn't it, that even as all this was happening—even as Jesus rode into Jerusalem—they saw Him but were blind to who He really was. They were looking for the Messiah. And in truth, here He was. But they were looking for the wrong messiah—and their disappointment would soon turn to rage.

Over in Luke is a parallel account of the events of that day. As the people and Christ's followers shouted their praises, the religious leaders grew increasingly angry. "And some of the Pharisees called to Him from the crowd, 'Teacher, rebuke Your disciples.' But He answered and said to them, 'I tell you that if these should keep silent, the stones would immediately cry out' " (Luke 19:39, 40).

"This is My time," Jesus was saying. Christ had avoided the public eye. On earlier occasions, He had stayed away from the people when they tried to make Him King. But now, He says, "This is My time." Then Jesus shared with the crowd a sobering prophecy. "Now as He drew near, He saw the city and wept over it, saying, 'If you had known, even you, especially in this your day, the things that make for your peace! But now they are hidden from your eyes. For days will come upon you when your enemies will build an embankment around you, surround you and close you in on every side, and level you, and your children within you, to the ground; and they will not leave in you one stone upon another, because you did not know the time of your visitation' " (verses 41–44).

He's looking down the line to A.D. 70, and Jesus says, "If only you knew. You want peace. But you're missing it." Here in their midst was the Prince of Peace—and they were completely missing Him. Here He was, the true Messiah of their prophecies and their fondest hopes—and they were missing Him. They missed Him because they didn't understand why He had come.

Perhaps in the crowd following Him along was Mary of Bethany. She didn't miss Him. There's Lazarus—he didn't miss Him. And there's Martha—she didn't miss Him; she understood. They all understood, but the great religious leaders missed Him, because they did not understand.

In college I always appreciated my English and literature teachers. Some of the greatest people I've ever known were the teachers who taught those subjects. Miss Andrews was my literature teacher at Keene, Texas, and later, when I went to Andrews University, I had a teacher named Harry Taylor. I appreciated him so much, not only as a teacher but as a person.

I remember my junior year there. It was test week, and I got a call that my dad had lung cancer. My dad had been very sick. I had been home to see him once earlier, during spring vacation. Now word came that Dad was in the hospital and would probably die in a short period of time. They told me that if I wanted to see him alive one more time, I should come now.

So I began preparing to go home. I went to see my teachers. This was just before the weekend, and test week was starting on Monday. Teacher after teacher said to me, "Certainly you can go, but just understand that sometime, you're going to have to come back here and make up these tests."

"Well," I said, "I've got summer employment out in Idaho with the Forest Service and I'll be going on to my summer job after visiting my dad. They tell me he won't live but a few days. So I don't know just when I'll be able to come back, but probably not before the end of the summer."

"We'll just put your grades in limbo," they said, "and we'll wait till you come back and take the tests at the end of summer."

Have you ever tried to take a test at the end of the summer on a course that you took back in the spring? It is not easy. When I went to see Harry Taylor, he said, "You don't have to take a test. You've already taken the course. You've got a good grade right now, and if you took the test, I think you would make the grade again. So I'm going to give you what you have right now as your grade."

I will never forget that man for that—for as long as I live! I will also never forget his classes. They were just great. One of the stories we looked at was "The Gift of the Magi" by O. Henry. The story is about two American young people, Jim and Della, and they are poor.

Christmastime comes around, and they want to give gifts to

each other. Della has long, beautiful hair. Jim wants to buy some special gift for her that would enhance that hair even more. He thinks of his gold watch. He doesn't have a chain for it—just sticks it in his pocket—but it's about his only treasure.

If you've heard the story, you know what happens. Della goes out, has her long hair cut off, and sells it for twenty dollars to a wigmaker. With that, she buys Jim a chain for his watch. Meanwhile, Jim takes his prized gold watch to a pawnshop and sells it for enough to buy Della a set of beautiful tortoiseshell combs she had longed for since seeing them in a storefront window.

They each give the other their gifts. Jim hands her the combs for her long hair—and she now has short hair. She gives him a watch chain for a watch that he no longer has—because he sold it for her. All we see is love. Love, one for another. When Jesus was on this earth, it's no wonder He spent so much time with Mary and Martha and Lazarus, because there He was loved.

Jesus gives His love even if it's never returned. But just because He gives love so freely does not mean He doesn't enjoy receiving it.

Of all the disciples, John most freely gave back the love he received from Jesus. His entire gospel story breathes the love these two shared. It's a story, a relationship, ready to be repeated between you and Jesus.

You love Jesus, without doubt.

How long since you've told Him so?

If you appreciated this book, you'll want to read other recent books by **James W. Gilley**:

KEEP ON KEEPING ON

Times are hard. The evening news is full of foreclosures, layoffs, rising prices, crime, natural disasters, global warming, contamination of food supplies, wars, epidemics, and more. No matter what your situation is, put your faith in God one day at a time. James W. Gilley, president of Three Angels Broadcasting Network, shares from his own experiences encouraging stories to strengthen your faith in God and help you keep on keeping on. Paperback, 160 pages.

ISBN 10: 0-8163-2059-4   ISBN 13: 978-0-8163-2059-2

THE BATTLE IS THE LORD'S
SPIRITUAL STRATEGIES FOR VICTORY IN YOUR DAILY STRUGGLES

When we think about enduring to the end, we focus on the "time of trouble." But our greatest challenge may be the enemy within. Fear, worry, stress, anxiety—these are just a few of the times of trouble we face on a daily basis. And they can wear us down if we're not careful. James Gilley points to the only successful way to face our daily times of trouble. Remember, we're not fighting the battle alone. In fact, it is not our fight at all. The battle is the Lord's! Paperback, 128 pages.

ISBN 10: 0-8163-1983-9   ISBN 13: 978-0-8163-1983-1

Three Ways to Order:
In Person: Local Adventist Book Center®
Call: 1-800-765-6955
Web site: AdventistBookCenter.com